Big Data Processing with Apache Spark

Efficiently tackle large datasets and big data analysis with Spark and Python

Manuel Ignacio Franco Galeano

Data Processing with Apache Spark

Author: Manuel Franco

Reviewer: Amit Nandi

Managing Editor: Edwin Moses

Acquisitions Editor: Aditya Date

Production Editor: Nitesh Thakur

Editorial Board: David Barnes, Ewan Buckingham, Simon Cox, Manasa Kumar, Alex Mazonowicz, Douglas Paterson, Dominic Pereira, Shiny Poojary, Saman Siddiqui, Erol Staveley, Ankita Thakur, and Mohita Vyas

First Published: October 2018

Production Reference: 1311018

ISBN: 978-1-78980-881-0

Table of Contents

Preface   i

Introduction to Spark Distributed Processing   1

Introduction 2

Introduction to Spark and Resilient Distributed Datasets 4

    Spark Components 5

    Spark Deployment Modes 5

    Spark Standalone 6

    Apache Mesos 6

    Other Deployment Options 7

    Resilient Distributed Datasets 7

    Python Shell and SparkContext 8

    Parallelized Collections 8

    RDD Creation from External Data Sources 9

    Exercise 1: Basic Interactive Analysis with Python 10

Operations Supported by the RDD API 12

    Map Transformations 12

    Reduce Action 13

    Working with Key-Value Pairs 13

    Join Transformations 13

    Set Operations 14

    Exercise 2: Map Reduce Operations 14

    Activity 1: Statistical Operations on Books 19

Self-Contained Python Spark Programs 20

    Introduction to Functional Programming 21

    Exercise 3: Standalone Python Programs 23

Introduction to SQL, Datasets, and DataFrames 27

    Exercise 4: Downloading the Reduced Version of the movielens Dataset . 28

    Exercise 5: RDD Operations in DataFrame Objects 31

Summary 32

Introduction to Spark Streaming   35

Introduction 36

Introduction to Streaming Architectures 36

    Back-Pressure, Write-Ahead Logging, and Checkpointing 38

Introduction to Discretized Streams 38

    Consuming Streams from a TCP Socket 39

    TCP Input DStream 39

    Map-Reduce Operations over DStreams 40

    Exercise 6: Building an Event TCP Server 41

    Activity 2: Building a Simple TCP Spark Stream Consumer 43

    Parallel Recovery of State with Checkpointing 44

    Keeping the State in Streaming Applications 45

    Join Operations 46

    Exercise 7: TCP Stream Consumer from Multiple Sources 47

    Activity 3: Consuming Event Data from Three TCP Servers 50

Windowing Operations 51

    Exercise 8: Distributed Log Server 51

Introduction to Structured Streaming 59

    Result Table and Output Modes in Structured Streaming 60

    Exercise 9: Writing Random Ratings 61

    Exercise 10: Structured Streaming 64

    Summary 65

Spark Streaming Integration with AWS   67

Introduction 68

Spark Integration with AWS Services 68

    Previous Requirements 68

    AWS Kinesis Data Streams Basic Functionality 69

Integrating AWS Kinesis and Python 70

    Exercise 11: Listing Existing Streams 70

    Exercise 12: Creating a New Stream 72

    Exercise 13: Deleting an Existing Stream 73

    Exercise 14: Pushing Data to a Stream 75

    AWS S3 Basic Functionality 77

    Creating, Listing, and Deleting AWS S3 Buckets 78

    Exercise 15: Listing Existing Buckets 78

    Exercise 16: Creating a Bucket 80

    Exercise 17: Deleting a Bucket 81

    Kinesis Streams and Spark Streams 83

    Activity 4: AWS and Spark Pipeline 84

    Summary 86

Spark Streaming, ML, and Windowing Operations   89

Introduction 90

Spark Integration with Machine Learning 90

    The MovieLens Dataset 90

    Introduction to Recommendation Systems and Collaborative Filtering 91

    Exercise 18: Collaborative Filtering and Spark 92

    Exercise 19: Creating a TCP Server that Publishes User Ratings 96

    Exercise 20: Spark Streams Integration with Machine Learning 99

    Activity 5: Experimenting with Windowing Operations 101

    Summary 102

Appendix A   105

Index   123

Preface

About

This section briefly introduces the author, the coverage of this course, the technical skills you'll need to get started, and the hardware and software requirements required to complete all of the included activities and exercises.

About the Book

Processing big data in real time is challenging due to scalability, information consistency, and fault-tolerance. Big Data Processing with Apache Spark teaches you how to use Spark to make your overall analytical workflow faster and more efficient. You'll explore all core concepts and tools within the Spark ecosystem, such as Spark Streaming, the Spark Streaming API, machine learning extension, and structured streaming.

You'll begin by learning data processing fundamentals using Resilient Distributed Datasets (RDDs), SQL, Datasets, and Dataframes APIs. After grasping these fundamentals, you'll move on to using Spark Streaming APIs to consume data in real time from TCP sockets, and integrate Amazon Web Services (AWS) for stream consumption.

By the end of this course, you'll not only have understood how to use machine learning extensions and structured streams but you'll also be able to apply Spark in your own upcoming big data projects.

About the Author

Manuel Ignacio Franco Galeano is a computer scientist from Colombia. He works for Fender Musical Instruments as a lead engineer in Dublin, Ireland. He holds a master's degree in computer science from University College, Dublin UCD. His areas of interest and research are music information retrieval, data analytics, distributed systems, and blockchain technologies.

Lesson Objectives

- Write your own Python programs that can interact with Spark
- Implement data stream consumption using Apache Spark
- Recognize common operations in Spark to process known data streams
- Integrate Spark streaming with Amazon Web Services
- Create a collaborative filtering model with Python and the MovieLens dataset
- Apply processed data streams to Spark machine learning APIs

Audience

Big Data Processing with Apache Spark is for you if you are a software engineer, architect, or IT professional who wants to explore distributed systems and big data analytics. Although you don't need any knowledge of Spark, prior experience of working with Python is recommended.

Approach

This course takes a hands-on approach to the practical aspects of data streaming with Spark. It contains multiple activities that use real-life business scenarios for you to practice and apply your new skills in a highly relevant context.

Minimum Hardware Requirements

For an optimal student experience, we recommend the following hardware configuration:

- Processor: Intel Core i5 or equivalent
- Memory: 4GB RAM
- Storage: 35 GB available space

Software Requirements

You'll also need the following software installed in advance:

- OS: Windows 7 SP1 64-bit, Windows 8.1 64-bit, or Windows 10 64-bit
- Python 3.0 or above
- Spark 2.3
- Amazon Web Services (AWS) account

Conventions

Code words in text, database table names, folder names, filenames, file extensions, pathnames, dummy URLs, user input, and Twitter handles are shown as follows: "map, filter, flatMap, union, intersection, distinct, groupByKey, and reduceByKey are functions used for transformations."

A block of code is set as follows:

```
filtered_words = distributed_words.filter(lambda x: len(x) > 3)
filtered_words.count()
```

New terms and important words are shown in bold. Words that you see on the screen, for example, in menus or dialog boxes, appear in the text like this: "Enter the receiver address in the **To Address** field."

Installation and Setup

Apache Spark is a general purpose framework for distributed computing. We will use the latest version that is available at the time of writing, which is version 2.3.0. Students require a local version of Spark running in their local environments. Installation guidelines can be found on the main Spark website at https://spark.apache.org/docs/latest/index.html#downloading.

Spark runs on Java 8, Python 2.7/3.4, R 3.1, and Scala 2.11. The language of choice for this course is Python 3.4.

Check your Python version: Spark uses Python 2.7 by default. Therefore, we need to specify the Python version we want to use by setting an environment variable:

```
export PYSPARK_PYTHON=python3
```

Some practical exercises require data from external sources, including the local filesystem and the internet. Other exercises require you to export data to the local filesystem. It is up to every student to choose the most convenient location for this directory.

The **$SPARK_DATA** environment variable specifies the data directory location.

The following example shows how to set the data variable to a local directory named data:

```
export SPARK_DATA=~/data
```

Some practical exercises require you to have the **$YOUR_SPARK_HOME** environment variable.

Additional Resources

The code bundle for this course is also hosted on GitHub at https://github.com/TrainingByPackt/Big-Data-Processing-with-Apache-Spark.

We also have other code bundles from our rich catalog of books and videos available at https://github.com/PacktPublishing/. Check them out!

1

Introduction to Spark Distributed Processing

Lesson Objectives

By the end of this chapter, you will be able to:

- Write Python programs that execute parallel operations inside a Spark cluster

- Create and transform resilient distributed datasets

- Write standalone Python programs to interact with Spark

- Build DataFrames and perform SQL queries

In this lesson, you will be interacting with Spark using Python.

Introduction

Apache Spark is a cluster computing framework that provides a collection of APIs. These APIs serve the purpose of performing general-purpose computation in clustered systems.

We can illustrate how Spark can be used in the real world with the example of a content provider that delivers movies, documentaries, and TV shows across the world. We'll call this service *MyContent*.

MyContent is deployed using the services of a cloud provider that has multiple data centers across the world, bringing to MyContent the possibility of optimizing the content delivery based on geolocalization.

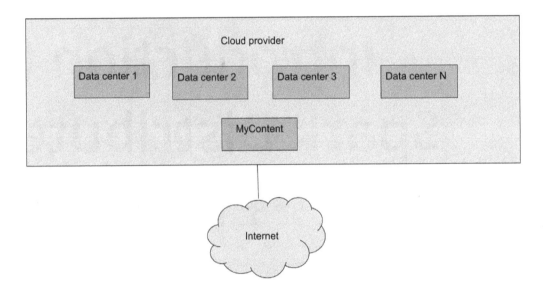

Figure 1.1: MyContent and cloud provider

The engineering and operations team at MyContent can use Spark to measure information, such as the locations that originate the most traffic at any time. This information can be used to update the computing consumption capacity in every data center, in order to optimize costs:

Figure 1.2: Accessing MyContent from devices.

Data scientists at MyContent can use Spark to measure the content that is being consumed by users around the world in real time and improve the recommendation system. A similar pipeline can be used for advertising and marketing:

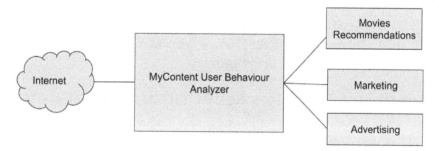

Figure 1.3: Pipeline for advertising and marketing.

Behind the scenes, both analyzers (geolocalization and user behavior) can be implemented by using one or more Spark components. The following diagram describes a scenario where Spark streaming is used to consume and aggregate information about users in real time. The aggregated data about geolocation is stored in a NoSQL database, whereas the information about user behavior is redirected to the Spark machine learning module, to improve a collaborative filtering model for movies recommendations:

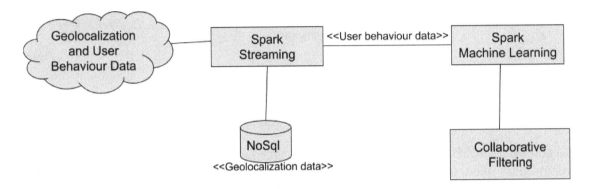

Figure 1.4: Geolocalization and user behavior.

In this lesson, you will learn about the basic concepts behind **resilient distributed datasets** (**RDD**), SQL, datasets, and DataFrames. You will also learn how to interact with Spark, using Python and functional programming.

Introduction to Spark and Resilient Distributed Datasets

Spark supports the following programming languages:

- Scala
- Java
- Python
- R
- SQL

> **Note**
>
> To learn more about how Spark supports these languages, you can go to https:// spark.apache.org/docs/latest/api/.

We'll use Python for the code examples in this course. Nevertheless, it should be relatively easy to migrate the code to another languages.

Spark Components

Having a good understanding of Spark components is essential for us to learn Spark. Here's a list of the Spark components:

- **Resilient distributed datasets**: This is an API that provides the functionality to perform operations in a distributed environment

- **SQL, DataFrames, and datasets**: This module contains interfaces to operate structured data

- **Streaming (DStreams)**: Extension for the distributed processing of live data streams

- **Machine Learning Library (MLlib)**: The collection of machine learning algorithms and utilities

- **GraphX**: Extensions that integrate graph-parallel computation

> **Note**
>
> For more information on Spark components, go to https://spark.apache.org/docs/latest/.

Spark Deployment Modes

Spark programs require a connection to a Spark cluster, in order to perform any computation.

SparkContext is the main entry point for Spark applications, and it represents a connection to the cluster that can be used to create RDDs and perform distributed computations:

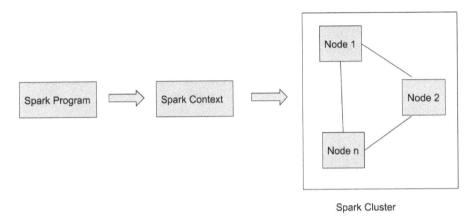

Figure 1.5: Spark Program and Spark Context

Spark Standalone

This mechanism provides an easy way to deploy a Spark cluster. All you need to do is place a copy of Spark in every machine inside the cluster.

This mode is suitable for local development, as the minimum number of nodes required is one.

> **Note**
>
> For relevant documentation about how to deploy a standalone cluster, go to
> https://spark.apache.org/docs/latest/spark-standalone.html.

Apache Mesos

Apache Mesos is an open source, general-purpose cluster manager. It provides some advantages compared to the standalone mode because Mesos can handle multiple instances of Spark, and is able to allocate shared resources across different platforms.

> **Note**
>
> To get information on how to run Spark on Mesos, go to https://spark.apache.org/
> docs/latest/running-on-mesos.html.

Other Deployment Options

Here are some of the other deployment options that are available:

- Apache Hadoop YARN (https://spark.apache.org/docs/latest/running-on-yarn.html)

- Kubernetes (https://spark.apache.org/docs/latest/running-on-kubernetes.html)

Resilient Distributed Datasets

Spark applications run a user's code and perform parallel operations in a distributed environment.

Spark's resilient distributed dataset is an abstraction that hides most of the complexity behind distributed computation, such as consistency of state and recovery from node failures. RDDs represent collections of elements that are distributed across different nodes in a cluster.

The consistency of state has proven to be a difficult problem to solve in distributed systems. Spark handles this problem by introducing the concept of shared variables. These types of variables can be used safely in parallel operations. The following diagram depicts a Spark cluster:

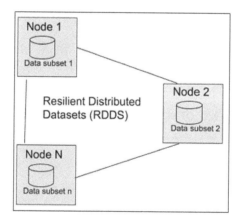

Figure 1.6: Data processing Spark cluster with RDDs on different nodes

Python Shell and SparkContext

Spark provides a Python interactive shell that can be used for quick and simple computations. This shell includes a SparkContext object that handles the connection to a Spark cluster. This context object can be used to create RDDs and broadcast variables.

The following command initiates a Python Spark session:

```
$YOUR_SPARK_HOME/bin/pyspark
```

After typing the preceding command, you should see an interactive shell very similar to the one shown in the following image:

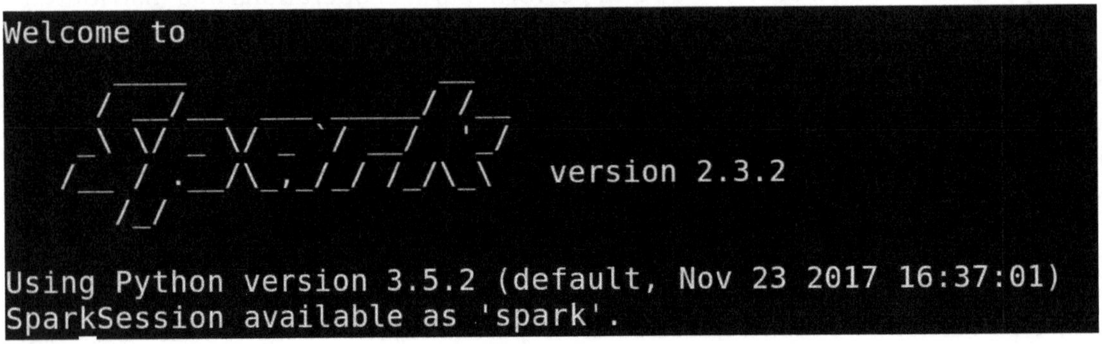

Figure 1.7: Python Spark session

Parallelized Collections

A **parallelized collection** represents a distributed dataset of items that can be operated in parallel, in different nodes in the Spark cluster.

The following example shows how to use the SparkContext object to create a parallelized collection from a list of words:

```
words = [
    'Apache', 'Spark', 'is', 'an', 'open-source', 'cluster-computing',
    'framework', 'Apache', 'Spark', 'open-source', 'Spark'
]
distributed_words = sc.parallelize(words)
```

Once the RDD has been created, it is possible to interact with it by performing different transformations and actions that are available in the Spark API.

The following example shows how to create a new RDD from the **distributed_words** dataset by excluding words with lengths that are less than three characters:

```
filtered_words = distributed_words.filter(lambda x: len(x) > 3)

filtered_words.count()
```

RDD datasets can be operated in parallel. An important parameter that can be used when creating parallelized collections is the number of partitions to split the dataset into. Spark executes one task in every partition; a common approach is to use between two and four partitions by CPU, although Spark attempts to set this number automatically.

The following example shows how to create a parallelized collection distributed across 8 partitions:

```
distributed_words2 = sc.parallelize(words, 8)
```

RDD Creation from External Data Sources

Spark supports the creation of RDDs from external sources, such as the local filesystem, databases, and Amazon S3, among others.

The following example creates a distributed dataset from a file located on the root for your Spark installation, and applies a basic transformation by excluding the words with a lengths shorter than three characters:

```
local_file = sc.textFile("README.md")

local_file.count()

local_file.filter(lambda x: len(x) > 3).count()
```

The following image summarizes the examples we have seen about RDDs and paralellized collections:

```
>>> words = [
...     'Apache', 'Spark', 'is', 'an', 'open-source', 'cluster-computing',
...     'framework', 'Apache', 'Spark', 'open-source', 'Spark'
... ]
>>>
>>> # Creates a RDD from a list of words
... distributed_words = sc.parallelize(words)
>>> distributed_words.count()
11
>>>
>>> # Creates a RDD by excluding words with length lower
... filtered_words = distributed_words.filter(lambda x: len(x) > 3)
>>> filtered_words.count()
9
>>>
>>> # Creates a parallelized collection splitted in 8 partitions
... distributed_words2 = sc.parallelize(words, 8)
>>> distributed_words2.count()
11
>>>
>>>
>>> # Creates a distributed dataset from a local file
... local_file = sc.textFile("README.md")
>>> local_file.count()
103
>>> local_file.filter(lambda x: len(x) > 3).count()
64
```

Figure 1.8: Output of the Examples

Exercise 1: Basic Interactive Analysis with Python

In this exercise, you will create an RDD from a sequence of 10,000 integers, to perform different filtering operations. We'll make use of the basic concepts about distributed processing in Spark with simple Python-based exercises.

Here are the steps to complete this exercise:

1. Create an RDD with numbers from -5,000 to 5,000.

    The following code shows how to create an RDD with numbers from -5,000 to 5,000. This dataset will be used in further steps to demonstrate basic RDD functionality:

    ```
    numbers = [x for x in range(-5000, 5000)]
    paralellized_numbers = sc.parallelize(numbers)
    paralellized_numbers.count()
    paralellized_numbers.first()
    paralellized_numbers.min()
    paralellized_numbers.max()
    ```

2. Create a new RDD with positive numbers:

```
# creates a new RDD with only positive numbers from the original dataset
positive_numbers = paralellized_numbers.filter(lambda x: x >= 0)
positive_numbers.count()
positive_numbers.first()
positive_numbers.min()
positive_numbers.max()
```

3. Write a Python function that returns true if a number is a multiple of 3; otherwise, it will return false.

It is possible to use normal functions and not Lambda functions to perform transformations from the original dataset:

```
def is_multiple(n):
    """
    returns true if a number is multiple of 3,
    otherwise returns false
    """
    if n % 3 == 0:
        return True
    else:
        return False
```

4. Create a new RDD with numbers that are multiples of 3:

```
# creates a new RDD with numbers multiple of 3
multiple_numbers = paralellized_numbers.filter(is_multiple)
multiple_numbers.count()
multiple_numbers.first()
multiple_numbers.min()
multiple_numbers.max()
```

Here's the output:

```
>>> # creates a new RDD with numbers multiple of 35
... multiple_numbers = paralellized_numbers.filter(
...     is_multiple)
>>> multiple_numbers.count()
3333
>>> multiple_numbers.first()
-4998
>>> multiple_numbers.min()
-4998
>>> multiple_numbers.max()
4998
>>>
```

Figure 1.9: Output displaying an RDD with numbers that are multiples of 3

We have learned the basis of distributed collections and how to create resilient distributed datasets. We also learned how to use the Python interactive console to perform simple operations such as RDDs, manipulations, and dataset creation from external sources (like the local filesystem). We will unveil the power behind the RDD API in the following topics.

Operations Supported by the RDD API

RDDs support two types of operations: transformations and actions.

A transformation receives an existing dataset as a parameter, and returns a new one after performing one or more computations. Transformations in Spark are lazy. This means that Spark does not execute any transformation until an action is called. `map`, `filter`, `flatMap`, `union`, `intersection`, `distinct`, `groupByKey`, and `reduceByKey` are functions used for transformations. `reduce`, `collect`, `count`, `first`, `take`, `takeSample`, `takeOrdered`, and `saveAsTextFile` are functions that fall under the category of actions.

Map Transformations

One example of a transformation is the `map` function, which creates a new dataset by applying some computations to an existing RDD.

The following example takes a list of words in lowercase and returns a collection of the same words in uppercase:

```
# creates a RDD from a list of words
words = [
    'Apache', 'Spark', 'is', 'an', 'open-source', 'cluster-computing',
    'framework', 'Apache', 'Spark', 'open-source', 'Spark'
]
distributed_words = sc.parallelize(words)
distributed_words.count()
distributed_words.first()
# applies a transformation that returns words RDD mapped to uppercase
upper_words = distributed_words.map(lambda x: x.upper())
upper_words.count()
upper_words.first()
```

Reduce Action

An action is a computation that returns a value after running one or more operations on the dataset. An example of an action is the **reduce** function, which takes two elements from the dataset and applies some computation.

The following example takes a list of words and returns a string with all of the words concatenated by commas:

```
distributed_words.reduce(lambda w1, w2:  w1 + ','  + w2)
```

Working with Key-Value Pairs

You can define a key-value pair by using a tuple in the format (key, value).

The following example shows you how to create two datasets from two collections of key-value pairs:

```
# simple key value examples
dataset1 = sc.parallelize(
    [('key1', 6), ('key2', 4), ('key7', 5), ('key10', 6)])
dataset2 = sc.parallelize(
    [('key1', 2), ('key3', 7), ('key8', 5), ('key10', 1)])


dataset1.first()
dataset2.first()
```

Join Transformations

Join transformations take two datasets and creates another one by joining the two initial datasets by key. You can use **leftOuterJoin, rightOuterJoin**, and **fullOuterJoin** to perform specific types of joins.

The following examples shows different types of joins:

```
dataset1.join(dataset2).take(10)
dataset1.leftOuterJoin(dataset2).take(10)
dataset1.rightOuterJoin(dataset2).take(10)
dataset1.fullOuterJoin(dataset2).take(10)
```

Set Operations

You can perform common set operations such as union and intersection between RDDs.

The following example shows how to apply these types of transformations:

```
# intersection  and union
set1 = sc.parallelize([1, 2, 3, 4, 5 ,6])
set2 = sc.parallelize([2, 4, 6, 8, 10])
set1.intersection(set2).collect()
set1.union(set2).collect()
```

Exercise 2: Map Reduce Operations

In this exercise, you will download two books from the Internet. You will build RDDs for every one of these books and you will perform a basic analysis for these two datasets.

You will learn about the most common operations for the creation and transformation of resilient distributed datasets (RDDs).

1. Create a RDD from text.

    The following code downloads a plain text version of the book A *Tale of Two Cities* by *Charles Dickens*, creates an RDD from it, and performs basics statistics such as count:

    ```
    sc.setLogLevel("ERROR")
    # downloads a plain text version of the book
    # "A Tale of Two Cities"
    import urllib.request
    url = 'https://raw.githubusercontent.com/maigfrga/spark-streaming-book/'\
          'master/data/books/tale2cities.txt'
    response = urllib.request.urlopen(url)
    data = response.read()
    data = data.decode('utf-8')
    # data is downloaded as very long string
    len(data)

    # split book in lines
    lines = data.split('\n')
    len(lines)

    # creates a RDD for the book
    ```

```
book = sc.parallelize(lines)
book.count()
book.first()
```

2. Perform dataset cleaning. Some cleaning tasks are required before we perform any computation in the dataset.

```
def clean_line(line):
    """
    Remove \ufeff\r characters
    Remove \t \n \r
    Remove additional characters
    """
    return line.replace('\ufeff\r', '').replace('\t', ' ').replace('\n',
'').\
        replace('\r', '').replace('(', '').replace(')', '').replace("'",
'').\
        replace('"', '').replace(',', '').replace('.', '').replace('*',
'')


# Remove characters and empty lines
cleaned_book = book.map(
    lambda x: clean_line(x)).filter(lambda x: x != '')
cleaned_book.count()
cleaned_book.first()
```

3. Tokenize and normalize the dataset.

Tokenization returns a list of all the words in the book, while normalization sets all tokens to lowercase. Use the **flatMap** function for this, which returns a sequence of items, as follows:

```
import redef normalize_tokenize(line):
    """
    Normalize: lowercase
    tokenize: split in tokens
    """
    return re.sub('\s+', ' ', line).strip().lower().split(' ')
tokens = cleaned_book.flatMap(normalize_tokenize)
tokens.count()
tokens.first()
```

4. Remove stop words.

   A stop word is a word that usually has a high frequency in the dataset, and does not provide any value, for example, the, a, as, and we. We assume for simplicity's sake that any word with a length less than or equal to 3 characters is a stop word, and will be removed:

   ```
   reduced_tokens = tokens.filter(lambda s: len(s) > 3)
   reduced_tokens.count()
   reduced_tokens.first()
   ```

5. Count the word frequency.

   The following code uses a map function to transform every token in the dataset into a tuple in the format **(token, 1)**. Then, we use the **reduceByKey** function to sum up all appearances by every token:

   ```
   counts = reduced_tokens.map(lambda x: (x, 1))
   counts.first()
   reduced_counts = counts.reduceByKey(
       lambda accumulator, value: accumulator + value)
   reduced_counts.take(4)

   # ordered by natural key (word)
   reduced_counts.takeOrdered(4)

   # ordered by frequency
   reduced_counts.takeOrdered(4, key=lambda x: x[1])

   # reverse order by frequency
   reduced_counts.takeOrdered(8, key=lambda x: -x[1])
   ```

6. Exclude the top frequency words.

   We can observe from the information collected in step 5 that the most frequent words are very generic (for example, that, they, with, then, there, them, and down). The following code removes the words with a frequency higher than 500:

   ```
   # 6 exclude top n words with top high frequency but meaningless
   twocities_book = reduced_counts.filter(lambda x: x[1] < 500)
   twocities_book.takeOrdered(8, key=lambda x: -x[1])
   ```

7. Process the *Hamlet* book.

    In this step, we will perform a basic analysis of *Hamlet*:

    ```python
    import urllib.request
    hamlet_url = 'https://raw.githubusercontent.com/maigfrga/spark-streaming-
    book/'\
        'master/data/books/hamlet.txt'
    response = urllib.request.urlopen(hamlet_url)
    data = response.read().decode('utf-8').split('\n')
    # Creates an RDD for the book
    # Removes characters, empty lines
    # Tokenize
    # Removes stop words
    # Counts frequency

    shakespeare_book = sc.parallelize(data).\
        map(lambda x: clean_line(x)).\
        filter(lambda x: x != '').\
        flatMap(normalize_tokenize).\
        filter(lambda s: len(s) > 3).\
        map(lambda x: (x, 1)).\
        reduceByKey(
            lambda accumulator, value: accumulator + value)

    shakespeare_book.count()
    shakespeare_book.first()

    # ordered by frequency
    shakespeare_book.takeOrdered(4, key=lambda x: x[1])

    # reverse order by frequency
    shakespeare_book.takeOrdered(8, key=lambda x: -x[1])

    hamlet_book = shakespeare_book.filter(lambda x: x[1] < 140)
    hamlet_book.takeOrdered(8, key=lambda x: -x[1])
    ```

8. Use a join transformation to find common words.

   We can use a join transformation to find out what words are common to both books:

   ```
   #8 Perform join operation to find out what words are used
   # in both books

   common_words = twocities_book.join(hamlet_book)
   common_words.count()



   # ordering by word
   common_words.takeOrdered(8)
   common_words.takeOrdered(8, key=lambda x: -1 * x[0])

   # ordering by the sum of the frequencies in both books
   common_words.takeOrdered(8, key=lambda x: x[1][0] + x[1][1])
   common_words.takeOrdered(8, key=lambda x: -1 * (x[1][0] + x[1][1]))
   ```

9. Find out what words are unique to one book or the other.

   A **leftOuterJoin** operation will create a dataset with words that exist in only one book:

   ```
   # words that are unique to twocities_book
   unique_twocities_book = twocities_book.\
       leftOuterJoin(hamlet_book).filter(lambda x: x[1][1] is None).\
       map(lambda x: x[0])

   unique_twocities_book.count()
   unique_twocities_book.take(6)

   # words that are unique to hamlet_book
   unique_hamlet_book = hamlet_book.\
       leftOuterJoin(twocities_book).filter(lambda x: x[1][1] is None).\
       map(lambda x: x[0])

   unique_hamlet_book.count()
   unique_hamlet_book.take(6)
   ```

Here's the output:

```
>>>
>>> unique_hamlet_book.count()
4304
>>> unique_hamlet_book.take(6)
['impond', 'serues', 'vneffectuall', 'colleagued', 'censure;', 'crab']
>>>
```

Figure 1.10: Output displaying words that are unique to a book

Activity 1: Statistical Operations on Books

In this activity, we'll do the following statistics on each of the books used in the previous exercise:

- Average length word.

- Standard deviation of average length word.

- Top 5 most frequent words in each book.

Prerequisites:

Use this function to get average word length:

```
avg =  book.map(lambda x: len(x[0]) ).reduce(operator.add) / book.count().
```

Use this function to get the standard deviation of average word length:

```
dev = statistics.stdev(
        book.map(
            lambda x: len(x[0])).collect()
```

Here are the steps to perform this activity:

1. Open the file you've used for the exercise (**book_analysis_act_b1.py** in this case).

2. Define a function by the name **statistics**, and import **operator** and **statistics**.

3. Next, get the average word length. Use the function mentioned in the *Prerequisites* section of this activity. Print the word length.

4. Next, get the standard deviation of average word length. Use the function mentioned in the *Prerequisites* section of this activity. Print it.

5. Print the most five frequent words in each book by using **book.takeOrdered(5, key=lambda k: -k[1])**.

> **Note**
>
> The solution for this activity can be found at Page No. 106.

In this section, we have learned how to use the RDD API to perform transformations and actions in numeric and text-based datasets. We explored a wide range of functionality that's provided by Spark, such as set operations, key value pairs, filtering, and mapping transformations, among others. We will learn how to create and execute standalone Python programs in the following activities. We will also revisit the basic concepts of Python functional programming.

Self-Contained Python Spark Programs

The interactive Python interface is a great tool for simple computations. Nevertheless, its functionality is limited even as the computing operations grow in complexity. In this section, we will learn how to write Python programs that can interact with a Spark cluster outside of the interactive console.

The following example is a very simple program called **check_python_version.py** that you can use to interact with Spark outside the console in the simplest possible way:

```python
import sys


from pyspark import SparkContext


if __name__ == "__main__":
    sc = SparkContext(appName="checkPythonVersion")
    sc.setLogLevel("ERROR")
    print(
        "Python version: {} Spark context version: {}".format(
            sys.version, sc.version))


sc.stop()
```

You can call the program with the following command (remember to define the **$YOUR_SPARK_HOME** variable, pointing to your local Spark installation):

```
YOUR_SPARK_HOME/bin/spark-submit --master local[4]  check_python_version.py
```

> For more information on the Spark Python API, you can check the Python API official documentation at https://spark.apache.org/docs/latest/api/python/index.html.

Introduction to Functional Programming

Now, you will learn about the basics of functional programming in Python. For an extensive guide, you can visit the official Python documentation at https://docs.python.org/3.5/howto/functional.html.

Lambda Functions

Lambda functions are statement functions that take 0 or more parameters and return a value. The aim of Lambda functions is simplicity. The return value is implicit; therefore, you cannot use the **return** keyword. The following code shows different examples of Lambda functions:

```
# square lambda function
square = lambda s: s**2
square(4)


# square anonymous lambda function
(lambda s: s**2)(4)


# creates a RDD and maps to square function
sc.parallelize([x for x in range(10)]).map(square).collect()


import random
# lambda function that takes an arbritrary number or strings and returns a string
# of comma-separated values
string_csv = lambda *args : ','.join(args)
string_csv('a', 'b', 'c')
```

```
string_csv(*[str(a) for a in range(10)])
# lambda function that returns a boolean
check_boolean = lambda  x: x > 20
check_boolean(1)
check_boolean(100)
# filter a sequence of numbers using a lambda function
sc.parallelize([x for x in range(30)]).filter(check_boolean).collect()
```

Nested Functions

Nested function are functions inside other functions. The most important advantage of this paradigm is that the outer scope cannot see what is happening in the inner function. Nonetheless, the inner scope can access variables in the outer scope.

The following code shows an example of a function that computes Fibonacci numbers using two approaches. Please note that there is a general function called Fibonacci, and there are two nested functions, one for each strategy:

```
def fibonacci(strategy, n):
    """
    Computes fibonacci using different strategies
    """
    def classic_fb(n):
        """
        Classic recursion approach
        """
        if n == 0: return 0
        elif n == 1: return 1
        else: return classic_fb(n - 1) + classic_fb(n - 2)
    def binet_fb(n):
        """
        Binet's Fibonacci Number Formula
        http://mathworld.wolfram.com/BinetsFibonacciNumberFormula.html
        """
        import math
        return (
```

```
                (1 + math.sqrt(5)) ** n -
                    ( 1 - math.sqrt(5)) ** n) / (2**n*math.sqrt(5))
        strategy_dict = {'classic': classic_fb, 'binet': binet_fb}
        return strategy_dict[strategy](n)



def benchmark_fibonacci():
    from datetime import datetime
    strategies = ('classic', 'binet')
    numbers = (10, 20, 30)
    for st in strategies:
        init = datetime.utcnow()
        for n in numbers:
            r = fibonacci(st, n)
            total_time = datetime.utcnow() - init
            print(
                'Strategy: {} result: {} n: {} execution time: {}'.format(
                    st, r, n, total_time
                ))
```

Exercise 3: Standalone Python Programs

In this exercise, you will refactor the code that we used in *Exercise 2, Map Reduce Operations* to create a standalone Python program that applies functional programming techniques to processes in text books. You will create standalone Python programs to perform analyses in Spark:

1. Create a Python file.

   Create a Python file called **book_analysis.py** and copy the following code:

   ```
   from pyspark import SparkContext


   def main():
       pass
   ```

```python
if __name__ == "__main__":
    sc = SparkContext(appName="bookAnalysis")
    sc.setLogLevel("ERROR")
    main()



    sc.stop()
```

2. Create a function to download text from the Internet that creates an RDD.

Add a new function to the Python script:

```python
def create_text_rdd_from_url(url):
    """
    Downloads content from a URL and
    creates a text based RDD
    """
    response = urllib.request.urlopen(url)
    data = response.read().decode('utf-8')
    lines = data.split('\n')
    # creates a RDD for the book
    return sc.parallelize(lines)
```

3. Create a function to clean a RDD that represents a book.

The **clean_book** function has two nested functions: one for removing characters and other one for normalizing and tokenizing:

```python
import re

def clean_book(book):
    def clean_line(line):
        """
        Remove \ufeff\r characters
        Remove \t \n \r
        Remove additional characters
        """
        return line.replace('\ufeff\r', '').\
            replace('\t', ' ').replace('\n', '').replace('\r', '').\
            replace('(', '').replace(')', '').replace("'", '').\
            replace('"', '').replace(',', ''). replace('.', '').\
            replace('*', '')

    def normalize_tokenize(line):
        """
```

```
    Normalize: lowercase
    tokenize: split in tokens
    """
    return re.sub('\s+', ' ', line).strip().lower().split(' ')

return book.map(lambda x: clean_line(x)).\
    filter(lambda x: x != '').flatMap(normalize_tokenize)
```

4. Remove any stop words:

```
def remove_stop_words(book):
    """
    Simple removal of words length less or equal to 3
    """
    return book.filter(lambda s: len(s) > 3)
```

5. Exclude the top *n* most popular words:

```
def exclude_popular_words(book, n):
    """
    Exclude top n most popular words
    """
    book = book.map(lambda x: (x, 1)).\
        reduceByKey(lambda accumulator, value: accumulator + value)
    cut_frequency = book.takeOrdered(8, key=lambda x: -x[1])[-1][1]
    return book.filter(lambda x: x[1] < cut_frequency)
```

6. Write a report generator with basic insights about the two books:

```
def report(book1, book2):
    unique_book1 = book1.\
        leftOuterJoin(book2).filter(lambda x: x[1][1] is None).\
        map(lambda x: x[0])

    print(
        "\n{} Words only exist in book {} ".format(
            unique_book1.count(), book1.name()))
    print( "Sample: {}".format(', '.join(unique_book1.take(5))) )

    unique_book2 = book2.\
        leftOuterJoin(book1).filter(lambda x: x[1][1] is None).\
        map(lambda x: x[0])

    print(
        "\n{} Words only exist in book {}".format(
```

```
                  unique_book2.count(), book2.name())))
        print( "Sample: {}".format(', '.join(unique_book2.take(5))) )

        common_words = book1.join(book2)
        print("\nCommon words in both books: {}".format(common_words.count()))
        print("Sample: {}".format(common_words.take(5)))
```

7. Create a function that processes the books *Tale of Two Cities* and *Hamlet*:

```
    def process_books():
        tale2cities_url = 'https://raw.githubusercontent.com/maigfrga/spark-
    streaming-book/'\
        'master/data/books/tale2cities.txt'

        hamlet_url = 'https://raw.githubusercontent.com/maigfrga/spark-
    streaming-book/'\
            'master/data/books/hamlet.txt'

        tale2cities = clean_book(create_text_rdd_from_url(tale2cities_url))
        tale2cities = remove_stop_words(tale2cities)
        tale2cities = exclude_popular_words(tale2cities, 10)
        tale2cities.setName('A tale of two cities')

        hamlet = clean_book(create_text_rdd_from_url(hamlet_url))
        hamlet = remove_stop_words(hamlet)
        hamlet = exclude_popular_words(hamlet, 10)
        hamlet.setName('hamlet')

        report(tale2cities, hamlet)

        report(huckleberry, hamlet)
```

8. Update the **main** function:

```
    def main():
        process_books()


    if __name__ == "__main__":
        sc = SparkContext(appName="bookAnalysis")
        sc.setLogLevel("ERROR")
        main()
```

9. Finally, run the analysis:

```
$YOUR_SPARK_HOME/bin/spark-submit --master local[4] book_analysis.py
```

```
[manuel@manuel-XPS-13-9350 ~]$ $YOUR_SPARK_HOME/bin/spark-submit --master local[4]  book_analy
sis.py

8524 Words only exist in book huckleberry
Sample: scooting, embattled, tools, subject, stoop

4306 Words only exist in book hamlet
Sample: impond, serues, vneffectuall, colleagued, censure;

Common words in both books: 1392
Sample: [('rotten', (5, 2)), ('hamlets', (3, 7)), ('right', (260, 11)), ('wild', (13, 2)), ('m
ichael', (2, 4))]
```

Figure 1.11: **Run analysis**

In this section, we have learned how to create standalone programs by using basic functional programming concepts. You can use these skills to extend the functionality provided by the interactive shell and perform complex analyses. In the following section, we will learn the basics of SQL and DataFrames.

Introduction to SQL, Datasets, and DataFrames

The Spark SQL API provides the functionality for storing and retrieving structured data. A dataset is a distributed collection that provides additional metadata about the structure of the data that is stored. The main difference between RDD and SQL datasets is that the former does not provide any information about the structure of the data. The metadata stored by datasets is used for internal optimizations.

A **DataFrame** is a dataset that organizes information into named columns. DataFrames can be built from different sources, such as JSON, XML, and databases.

The dataset API is only available for Java and Scala; nevertheless, it is possible to use Python to build and operate DataFrames.

For the remainder of this lesson, we will use the reduced version of the movielens dataset that contains 100,000 ratings and 1,300 tag applications, which have been applied to 9,000 movies by 700 users.

> **Note**
>
> Further information about this dataset can be found at https://grouplens.org/datasets/movielens/. **Reminder**: Before continuing, we will download a dataset from the Internet to the **$SPARK_DATA** location. If you have not defined this **environ** variable yet, you should do it now, otherwise, the Python code will throw an exception. This example shows how to set the data variable to a local directory: **export SPARK_DATA=~/data.**

Exercise 4: Downloading the Reduced Version of the movielens Dataset

In this exercise, we will write a Python 3 program that will run outside of the Spark environment. Generate a local copy of the movielens dataset.

Follow these steps to complete this exercise:

1. Create a file named **dowload_movielens.py**.

    Copy the following Python code that downloads the movilens dataset:

    ```python
    import urllib.request
    import os


    URLS = (
        'https://raw.githubusercontent.com/maigfrga/spark-streaming-book/master/data/movielens/tags.csv',  # noqa
        'https://raw.githubusercontent.com/maigfrga/spark-streaming-book/master/data/movielens/ratings.csv',  # noqa
        'https://raw.githubusercontent.com/maigfrga/spark-streaming-book/master/data/movielens/movies.csv'  # noqa,
    )

    def main():
    ```

```
"""
Download the reduced version of movielens dataset
"""

def download(url):
    response = urllib.request.urlopen(url)
    data = response.read()
    data = data.decode('utf-8')
    fname = url.split('/')[-1]
    with open(os.path.join(
            os.environ['SPARK_DATA'], fname), 'w') as f:
        f.write(data)

for url in URLS:
    download(url)


if __name__ == '__main__':
    if 'SPARK_DATA' not in os.environ:
        print('Error. Please define SPARK_DATA variable')
        exit(1)
    main()
```

2. Download the dataset.

You can now execute the Python code by running the following:

```
python3 dowload_movielens.py
```

Note

Please note that you don't need to be inside of a **pyspark** session to run this script.

Creating a DataFrame from a CSV File

The **pyspark.sql.dataframe.DataFrame** object represents a collection of **pyspark.sql.types.Row** objects.

The following code creates a **pyspark.sql.dataframe.DataFrame** object from a .csv file:

```
import os
fname = os.path.join(
                os.environ['SPARK_DATA'], 'movies.csv')


movies = spark.read.csv(
    fname, header=True, mode="DROPMALFORMED"
)


type(movies)
type(movies.first())
movies
movies.count()
movies.columns
movies.show()
```

Basic Queries in DataFrames

You can use the Spark SQL API to perform queries and functions in DataFrames.

The following example shows the basic usage of the SQL API:

```
# Selecting columns from dataset
movies.select('genres').show(5)
movies.select('movieId', 'genres').show(5)


# Filtering ids
movies.filter(movies['movieId'] > 5).show(5)
```

Running Queries from a Temporary View

You can create a temporary view from a DataFrame and perform SQL queries, like so:

```
movies.createOrReplaceTempView("movies")

movies2 = spark.sql("SELECT * FROM movies WHERE movieId > 10 AND movieId <
20")

movies2.show()
```

Exercise 5: RDD Operations in DataFrame Objects

In this exercise, we will transform the movies DataFrame by using RDD operations. We will perform string transformation.

The following are the steps for performing this exercise:

1. Access RDD functionality from a DataFrame.

    Every **pyspark.sql.dataframe.DataFrame** has an RDD object that represents an RDD version of the DataFrame:

    ```
    sc.setLogLevel("ERROR")
    movies_rdd = sc.parallelize(movies.select('movieId', 'genres').collect())
    movies_rdd.count()
    movies_rdd.first()
    ```

2. Transform the genres from a string to a list.

    The original dataset defines all genres of a movie as a string of values, separated by the special character "|". The following transformation splits this value and returns a list of genres by movie:

    ```
    movies.rdd.map(lambda row: (row['movieId'], row['genres'].split('|'))).
    first()
    ```

```
>>>
>>> movies.rdd.map(
...      lambda row:
...         (row['movieId'], row['genres'].split('|'))).first()
('1', ['Adventure', 'Animation', 'Children', 'Comedy', 'Fantasy'])
>>>
```

Figure 1.11: Output displaying the genres transformed from a string to a list

Summary

In this lesson, we have learned how to write Python programs to execute parallel operations inside of a Spark cluster. We also learned how to create and transform resilient distributed datasets from the interactive console, and wrote standalone Python programs to interact with Spark. We then explored the basic concepts of DataFrames and SQL queries.

In the following lesson, we will learn the most basic concepts regarding Spark Streaming.

Introduction to Spark Streaming

Lesson Objectives

By the end of this lesson, you will be able to:

- Explain the basic concepts behind streaming architectures
- Work with the most relevant operations for stream consumption
- Write Python Spark programs to consume streams of data in real time from TCP sockets
- Implement a basic pipeline to consume, aggregate, and store data in real time

This lesson focuses connecting to live data streams and processing them.

Introduction

In the previous lesson, we learned how to write Python programs to execute parallel operations inside a Spark cluster, and we created and transformed RDDs.

In this lesson, we will learn how to process streams of data in real time. You will write Python standalone programs for connecting to live streams of data by using similar concepts to those learned in *Lesson 1, Introduction to Distributed Processing with Spark*. You will also implement an end-to-end pipeline by the end of this lesson.

Introduction to Streaming Architectures

Consuming live streams of data has proven to be a challenging endeavor. One of the reasons why this consumption is difficult is the unpredictability of the volume of the incoming data. The variability in the flow of information may lead to situations where very fast producers may overwhelm consumers. Finding the right balance between reads and writes has proven to be difficult. The following image describes a system that consume information from multiple sources and performs transformations and aggregations before storage.

The following image describes a system that consumes information from multiple sources and performs transformations and aggregations before the information is stored.

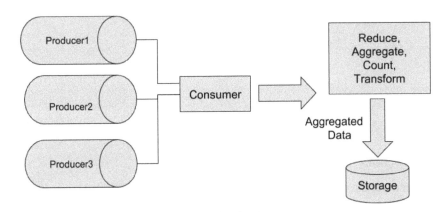

Figure 2.1: System with multiple sources

The following image describes a scenario where the system is idle most of the time because the amount of incoming data is very low. This scenario may lead to unnecessary allocation of computational power that otherwise can be used for more important tasks. Only one of the three producers are sending data to the system.

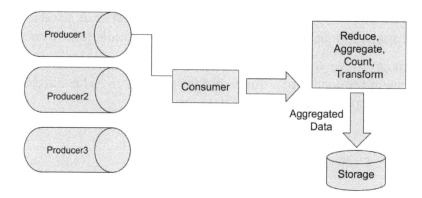

Figure 2.2: Idle system

Sometimes, the incoming data volume is higher than the ability of the consumer to process data. Consumers should implement mechanisms to handle this scenario, otherwise data loss will be unavoidable. The following image describes a scenario where the amount of consumers increases in a way that the producer is not able to handle all incoming data:

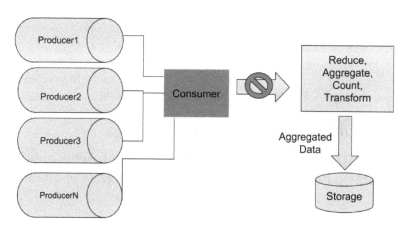

Figure 2.3: System with multiple producers and one consumer

Back-Pressure, Write-Ahead Logging, and Checkpointing

Back-pressure is a mechanism used in distributed systems to handle loads as they increase. Implementations of this technique may vary in different ways, nevertheless, the basic principles remains the same.

A mechanism known as **write-ahead logging** helps back-pressure by serializing all requests before further processing. Checkpointing is a technique used in distributed systems to take snapshots of the state of the system to handle failure recovery.

The following image shows a back pressure implementation where the consumer stores all processing request in to a queue before processing. The state of the system is serialized using checkpointing to prevent data loss.

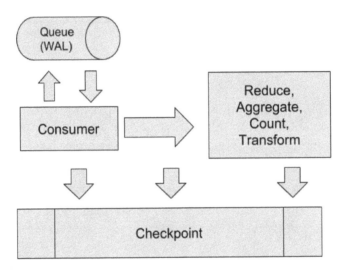

Figure 2.4 System with checkpointing

Introduction to Discretized Streams

Discretized Streams (**DStreams**) is an abstraction that represents continuous streams of data. This abstraction provides functionality for consistency and fault recovery.

The ability to perform parallel recovery of state represents an important innovation in comparison to traditional replication systems. DStreams also provides stragglers mitigation mechanisms.

> **Note**
>
> The paper that describes this specification can be found at https://www2.eecs. berkeley.edu/Pubs/TechRpts/2012/EECS-2012-259.pdf.

Consuming Streams from a TCP Socket

Spark Streaming is an extension of the core Spark API that groups incoming data into batches of Resilient Distributed Datasets RDDs. Each one of those batches contains data from a certain time interval.

The following diagram shows how Spark Streaming connects to a TCP server to process and store live data:

Figure 2.5 Spark Streaming and a TCP server

Spark Streaming receives streams of data in real time and splits this data into chunks or batches. Every batch is transformed by the Spark engine to an RDD.

TCP Input DStream

TCP Input DStreams represent streams of input data that are received from a TCP server. You must create a **pyspark.streaming.StreamingContext** object to connect to a stream:

```
spark_context = SparkContext(appName='LogSocketConsumer')
stream_context = StreamingContext(spark_context, interval)
```

The **socketTextStream** function from the **stream_context** object creates a TCP DStream:

```
stream = stream_context.socketTextStream(host, port)
```

Map-Reduce Operations over DStreams

Map-Reduce operations can be executed on DStreams. The following example performs a series of transformations over a DStream to finally apply the **reduceByKey** operation to every DStream to aggregate the amount of events in a given period of time:

```python
def parse_entry(msg):
    """

    Event TCP sends sends data in the format

    timestamp:event\n
    """

    values = msg.split(';')

    return {
        'dt': datetime.strptime(
            values[0], '%Y-%m-%d %H:%M:%S.%f'),
        'event': values[1]
    }


def aggregate_by_event_type(record):
    """

    Step 1. Maps every entry to a dictionary.

    Step 2. Transform the dataset in a set of
        tuples (event, 1)

    Step 3: Applies a reduction by event type
        to count the number of events by type
        in a given interval of time.
    """

    return record.map(parse_entry)\
        .map(lambda record: (record['event'], 1))\
        .reduceByKey(lambda a, b: a+b)
event_counts = aggregate_by_event_type(stream)
event_counts.pprint()
```

Exercise 6: Building an Event TCP Server

In this exercise, you will write a Python TCP server that sends random events across the network. Every record contains a timestamp and event type. You will implement a very simple mechanism to simulate non-deterministic delays between records.

Here are the steps to perform this exercise:

1. Create a Python file named **event_producer.py** and copy the following code:

```python
from pyspark import SparkContext
from pyspark.streaming import StreamingContext
from datetime import datetime

import argparse
import random
import time
import socket
```

2. Write a function to generate a string representing a random event. It must return a string with the current timestamp and a random event chosen from a list of events at random:

```python
def get_line():
    random.seed(datetime.utcnow().microsecond)
    dt = datetime.utcnow()\
        .strftime('%Y-%m-%d %H:%M:%S.%f')
    event = random.choice(['event1', 'event2', 'event3'])
    return '{};{}\n'.format(dt, event).encode('utf-8')
```

3. Write a function to create a random number. The aim of this number generation is to simulate a non-deterministic interval of time:

```python
def randomize_interval(interval):
    """
    Returns a random value sligthly different
    from the original interval parameter
    """
    random.seed(datetime.utcnow().microsecond)
    delta = interval + random.uniform(-0.1, 0.9)
    # delay can not be 0 or negative
    if delta <= 0:
        delta = interval
    return delta
```

4. Write a TCP socket server that sends a stream of events. Initialize a TCP server that returns a non-deterministic flow of simulated events to its clients:

```python
def initialize(port=9876, interval=0.5):
    sock = socket.socket(socket.AF_INET, socket.SOCK_STREAM)
    server_address = ('localhost', port)
    sock.bind(server_address)
    sock.listen(5)
    print("Listening at {}".format(server_address))
    try:
        connection, client_address = sock.accept()
        print('connection from', client_address)
        while True:
            line = get_line()
            connection.sendall(line)
            time.sleep(randomize_interval(interval))
    except Exception as e:
        print(e)

    finally:
        sock.close()
```

5. Use a main function that parse arguments that are used to initialize the server:

```python
def main():
    parser = argparse.ArgumentParser()
    parser.add_argument(
        '--port', required=False, default=9876,
        help='Port', type=int)

    parser.add_argument(
        '--interval', required=False, default=0.5,
        help='Interval in seconds', type=float)

    args, extra_params = parser.parse_known_args()
    initialize(port=args.port, interval=args.interval)


if __name__ == '__main__':
    main()
```

6. The following command initializes a TCP server in port 9875 that will send a message about a random event to clients in an interval close to 0.05 seconds:

```
python3 event_producer.py --interval 0.05 --port 9875
```

In this exercise, we implemented a very simple mechanism to simulate non-deterministic delays between records.

Activity 2: Building a Simple TCP Spark Stream Consumer

In this activity, you will write a Python program that consumes live streams of data from a TCP server. You will perform basic transformations and one aggregation by every chunk of data that arrives.

The aim of this activity is to implement a basic workflow for stream consumption of data in real time. You'll finally pull a live stream of data from a port, and build chunks of data that arrive in an interval within 3 seconds.

Here are the steps to perform this activity:

1. Create a Python file named event_stream_consumer.py and import the required libraries.

2. Next, write the function to parse a string event. The TCP server we implemented in this exercise pushes stream messages in the format **"timestamp;event\n"**. The function you write should parse strings in this format and return a dictionary.

3. Write a function that applies a series of transformations and actions to aggregate streams of data by event type.

4. Write a function that uses the Spark streams API to pull data from a socket in a given interval of time.

5. Write a simple Python 3 function that parses console arguments to provide an interface to users.

6. Use the command that connects to the TCP socket described in the preceding exercise, pulling a live stream of data from port 9875, and building chunks of data that arrive within an interval within 3 seconds.

> **Note**
>
> The solution for this activity can be found at page Page No. 107.

Now, you can experiment with different interval values from both the TPC Server and the Spark Consumer.

Operations Supported by the Spark Streaming API

Operations such as `map`, `flatMap`, `filter`, `union`, `count`, `repartition`, `reduce`, `countByValue`, `reduceByKey`, `join`, `cogroup`, and **transform** are equivalent to those in the RDD API. Additionally, there are operations that are exclusive to the Spark Streaming API, such as `updateStateByKey`.

Parallel Recovery of State with Checkpointing

Resilience to failures is a feature that distributed systems must provide. Being able to avoid experience complications such as network and system failures during the operation of a cluster isn't possible

The unavailability (temporary or definitive) of one or more nodes in a distributed environment will happen at some point in production environments.

Spark has implemented a checkpoint mechanism to write data to a fault tolerant storage system. Both metadata and data may be checkpointed. Metadata keeps the state of the computation being performed, while data stores information about RDDs.

Stateful transformations such as **updateStateByKey** or **reduceByKeyAndWindow** require checkpointing activation. This activation can be done by using the **streamingContext.checkpoint(checkpointDirectory)** function. The following code initializes a **SparkContext** and a **StreamingContext** with checkpoint enabled:

```
from pyspark import SparkContext
from pyspark.streaming import StreamingContext


spark_context = SparkContext(appName='TCPSocketConsumer')
stream_context = StreamingContext(spark_context, 10)
stream_context.checkpoint('/tmp')
```

Keeping the State in Streaming Applications

The **updateStateByKey** operation may be used to keep the state of a stream across different chunks of data. This operation receives, as a parameter, a function that will be applied to every key in the dataset. If the function returns **None** for a given key, this key-value pair will be eliminated. The following function receives a key-value pair dataset as a parameter and performs a **updateStateByKey** operation that sums all values by key:

```python
def update_global_event_counts(key_value_pairs):
    """

    Function that receives as parameter a DStream

    and applies an update function in order to keep

    aggregated information about event types counts.
    """

    def update(new_values, accumulator):
        if accumulator is None:
            accumulator = 0
        return sum(new_values, accumulator)
    return key_value_pairs.updateStateByKey(update)
```

The following code applies the **update_global_event_counts** function to the TCP stream dataset:

```python
key_value_pairs = stream.map(parse_entry)\
    .map(lambda record: (record['event'], 1))
running_event_counts = update_global_event_counts(key_value_pairs)
running_event_counts.pprint()
```

Join Operations

Join operations including `leftOuterJoin`, `rightOuterJoin`, and `fullOuterJoin` are supported by the streaming API. The following code creates two streams and transforms every stream in a key-value dataset:

```
stream = stream_context.socketTextStream('localhost', 98765)

stream2 = stream_context.socketTextStream('localhost', 12345)

key_value_pairs = stream.map(parse_entry).map(lambda record:
(record['event'], 1))

key_value_pairs2 = stream2.map(parse_entry).map(lambda record:
(record['event'], 1))
```

We can aggregate the number of events by event type for every stream:

```
running_event_counts = update_global_event_counts(key_value_pairs)

running_event_counts2 = update_global_event_counts(key_value_pairs2)
```

The following code joins two DStreams that contain event counts:

```
n_counts_joined = running_event_counts.leftOuterJoin(running_event_counts2)

n_counts_joined.pprint()
```

The joined vales can be transformed once more so that we can have a global aggregation from both streams:

```
def aggregate_joined_stream(pair):
    key = pair[0]
    values = [val for val in pair[1] if val is not None]
    return(key, sum(values))


n_counts_joined.map(aggregate_joined_stream)
```

Exercise 7: TCP Stream Consumer from Multiple Sources

In this exercise, you will write a Spark Python program that consumes live streams of data from a TCP server that is running in two different ports.

You will join both sources and perform basic transformations. The aim of this exercise is to apply Spark stream operations over multiple sources.

The following diagram describes the workflow that will be implemented:

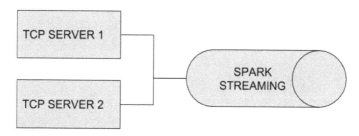

Figure 2.6: Workflow of TCP Stream consumer for multiple sources

Here are the steps to perform this exercise:

1. Create a file named **event_stream_stateful_consumer.py** and import the necessary packages:

    ```
    from datetime import datetime
    from pyspark import SparkContext
    from pyspark.streaming import StreamingContext
    import argparse
    ```

2. Create a main function to parse console parameters and initialize streams:

    ```
    def main():
        parser = argparse.ArgumentParser()
        parser.add_argument(
            '--interval', required=False, default=1.0,
            help='Interval in seconds', type=float)

        parser.add_argument(
            '--port1', required=False, default=9876,
            help='Port', type=int)
    ```

```
        parser.add_argument(
            '--port2', required=False, default=12345,
            help='Port', type=int)

        parser.add_argument(
            '--host', required=False, default='localhost', help='Host')

        args, extra_params = parser.parse_known_args()
        consume_records(
            interval=args.interval, port1=args.port1,
            port2=args.port2, host=args.host)


    if __name__ == '__main__':
        main()
```

3. Write a function to initialize SparkContext and StreamingContext with checkpoint enabled:

```
    def initialize_context(interval=1, checkpointDirectory='/tmp'):
        """
        Creates a SparkContext, and a StreamingContext object.
        Initialize checkpointing
        """

        spark_context = SparkContext(appName='LogSocketConsumer')
        stream_context = StreamingContext(spark_context, interval)
        stream_context.checkpoint(checkpointDirectory)
        return spark_context, stream_context
```

4. Write a function to initialize streams and start the computation:

```
    def consume_records(
            interval=1, host='localhost', port1=9876, port2=12345):
        """
        Create a local StreamingContext with two working    thread and batch
    interval
        """

        sc, stream_context = initialize_context(interval=interval)
        stream1 = stream_context.socketTextStream(host, port1)
        stream2 = stream_context.socketTextStream(host, port2)
        join_aggreation(stream1, stream2)
        stream_context.start()
        stream_context.awaitTermination()
```

5. Write a function that receives a DStream and updates its global state:

```python
def update_global_event_counts(key_value_pairs):
    def update(new_values, accumulator):
        if accumulator is None:
            accumulator = 0
        return sum(new_values, accumulator)

    return key_value_pairs.updateStateByKey(update)
```

6. Write the following function, which parses, joins, and aggregates two streams:

```python
def aggregate_joined_stream(pair):
    key = pair[0]
    values = [val for val in pair[1] if val is not None]
    return(key, sum(values))


def join_aggregation(stream1, stream2):
    key_value_pairs = stream1.map(parse_entry)\
        .map(lambda record: (record['event'], 1))
    running_event_counts = update_global_event_counts(key_value_pairs)
    running_event_counts.pprint()
    key_value_pairs2 = stream2.map(parse_entry)\
        .map(lambda record: (record['event'], 1))
    running_event_counts2 = update_global_event_counts(key_value_pairs2)
    running_event_counts2.pprint()
    n_counts_joined = running_event_counts.leftOuterJoin(running_event_
counts2)
    n_counts_joined.pprint()
    n_counts_joined.map(aggregate_joined_stream).pprint()
```

7. Execute the following command in your terminal to start a TCP server that sends event data in port 9876:

```
python3 event_producer.py --port 9876
```

8. Open another terminal and run the same command in a different port:

```
python3 event_producer.py --port 12345
```

9. Open a third terminal and run the Spark stream program:

```
$YOUR_SPARK_HOME/bin/spark-submit \
  --master local[4] \
   event_stream_stateful_consumer.py \
   --interval 3
```

This is how your output will look:

```
[manuel@manuel-XPS-13-9350 ~]$ $YOUR_SPARK_HOME/bin/spark-submit \
>    --master local[4] \
>     event_stream_stateful_consumer.py \
>     --interval 3
---------------------------------------------
Time: 2018-07-14 20:30:39
---------------------------------------------
```

Figure 2.7: Output with interval 3

Activity 3: Consuming Event Data from Three TCP Servers

In this activity, you will initialize a third TCP server. You will create another Python Spark program that consumes event data from three TCP servers instead of two. You will perform join transformations from multiple sources and aggregate data in order to compute a global count of events.

Here are the steps to perform this activity:

1. Create a Python file and import the required libraries, such as datetime, SparkContext, StreamingContext, and argparse.

2. Write a function by which Event TCP sends data in the format timestamp:event\n.

3. Write a function that maps every entry to a dictionary, transforms the dataset in a set of tuples (event, 1), and applies a reduction by event type to count the number of events by type in a given interval of time.

4. Write a function that receives as parameter a DStream and applies an update function in order to keep aggregated information about event types counts.

5. Write a function that parses, joins, and aggregates three streams.

6. Write a function that creates a local StreamingContext with two working thread and batch interval.

7. Write a function that creates a SparkContext, and a StreamingContext object. Initialize checkpointing as well.

8. Write a main function to parse console parameters and initialize streams.

9. Run the program.

> **Note**
>
> The solution for this activity can be found at Page No. 109.

Windowing Operations

Spark Streams provides an interface to apply computations to sliding windows of data. The following image describes a scenario where streams of data are grouped in windows of 3 streams every 2 time units:

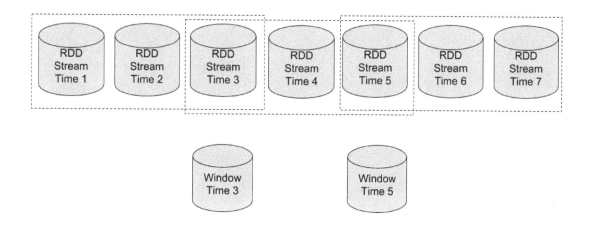

Figure 2.8: Windowing Operations

Exercise 8: Distributed Log Server

In this exercise, you will write a TCP server that simulates log entries from a web server. You will instantiate multiple instances of this server to send log data to Spark in a distributed manner.

We'll apply the concepts from lessons 1 and 2 to implement an end-to-end pipeline for data consumption and processing in real time.

The Proposed Architecture

Here, we will propose the implementation of a TCP server that will send log entries to Spark Streaming from three different ports. Spark will process the streams in real time and apply transformations.

In the last step of processing, Spark will write aggregated data to the filesystem.

Creating a TCP Server

Here are the steps to create a TCP server:

1. Create a file named **log_socket_producer.py**, and copy the following imports and global variables:

```python
from datetime import datetime
import argparse
import random
import time
import socket

HTTP_CODES = (
    200, 201, 300, 301, 302, 400, 401, 404, 500, 502
)


PATHS = (
    '/', '/home', '/login', '/user', '/user/profile',
    '/user/network/friends'
)

AGENTS = (
    'Mozilla/5.0 (Windows NT 6.1; WOW64; rv:40.0) Gecko/20100101
Firefox/40.1',
    'Mozilla/5.0 (Windows NT 6.3; rv:36.0) Gecko/20100101 Firefox/36.0',
    'Mozilla/5.0 (Windows NT 5.1) AppleWebKit/537.36 (KHTML, like Gecko)'
    'Chrome/41.0.2224.3 Safari/537.36',
    'EsperanzaBot(+http://www.esperanza.to/bot/)',
    'Mozilla/5.0 (compatible; bingbot/2.0; +http://www.bing.com/bingbot.
htm)'
)
```

2. Create a function to generate a random entry that simulates an http request to a web server:

```python
def get_data():
    """

    Similates a log entry for a webserver in the format
    $remote_addr - [$time_local] "$request" $status $body_bytes_sent
    $http_user_agent"
    """

    random.seed(datetime.utcnow().microsecond)
    data = {}
    data['ip'] = '{0}.{1}.{2}.{3}'.format(
        random.randint(0, 255), random.randint(0, 255), random.randint(0,
255),
        random.randint(0, 255))

    data['time'] = datetime.utcnow()
    data['request'] = random.choice(PATHS)
    data['status'] = random.choice(HTTP_CODES)
    data['bytes'] = random.randint(1, 2048)
    data['agent'] = random.choice(AGENTS)
    return data


def get_line():
    base = '{ip} - [{time}] "{request}" {status} {bytes} "{agent}"\n'
    data = get_data()
    return base.format(**data)
```

3. Write a function that initializes a TCP server that sends log entries to its consumers:

```python
def initialize(port=9876, interval=0.5):
    """

    Establish a connection with a stream socket consumer
    and push simulated log entries.
    """

    sock = socket.socket(socket.AF_INET, socket.SOCK_STREAM)
    server_address = ('localhost', port)
    print("Listening at {}".format(server_address))
    sock.bind(server_address)
    sock.listen(5)
    try:
        connection, client_address = sock.accept()
```

```python
        print('connection from', client_address)
        while True:
            line = get_line().encode('utf-8')
            connection.sendall(line)
            print(line)
            time.sleep(interval)
    except Exception as e:
        print(e)

    finally:
        sock.close()
```

4. Write the main function that starts the server:

```python
def main():
    """
    Push data to a TCP socket
    """
    parser = argparse.ArgumentParser()
    parser.add_argument(
        '--port', required=False, default=9876,
        help='Port', type=int)

    parser.add_argument(
        '--interval', required=False, default=0.5,
        help='Interval in seconds', type=float)

    args, extra_params = parser.parse_known_args()
    initialize(port=args.port, interval=args.interval)


if __name__ == '__main__':
    main()
```

5. Write a command to start the TCP server in port 12345:

```
python3 log_socket_producer.py --port 12345
```

6. Open another two windows and start another two instances of this server in ports 9876 and 8765.

Creating a TCP Spark Stream Consumer

1. Create a Python file named **log_socket_producer.py** and import the necessary packages and global variables:

```
from pyspark import SparkContext
from pyspark.streaming import StreamingContext
import argparse
import re
import os
```

2. Write a function that applies a regular expression to every incoming message and returns a dictionary:

```
def parse_log_entry(msg):
    """
    Parse a log entry from the format
    $ip_addr - [$time_local] "$request" $status $bytes_sent $http_user_
agent"
    to a dictionary
    """
    data = {}

    # Regular expression that parses a log entry
    search_term = '(\d{1,3}\.\d{1,3}\.\d{1,3}\.\d{1,3})\s+\-\s+\[(.*)]\
s+'\
        '"(\/[/.a-zA-Z0-9-]+)"\s+(\d{3})\s+(\d+)\s+"(.*)"'

    values = re.findall(search_term, msg)

    if values:
        val = values[0]
        data['ip'] = val[0]
        data['date'] = val[1]
        data['path'] = val[2]
        data['status'] = val[3]
        data['bytes_sent'] = val[4]
        data['agent'] = val[5]
    return data
```

3. Join the streams, apply basic cleaning, and return a key-value dataset by column:

```
def aggregate_by_column(
        stream1, stream2, stream3, column_name='path'):

    def transform(record):
        return record.map(parse_log_entry).filter(lambda record: record)\
        .map(lambda record: (record[column_name], record))

    def clean(record):
        key = record[0]
        value = tuple(
            x for x in record[1][0] if x
        )
        return (key, value)

    # Join streams
    joined_stream = transform(stream1)
.leftOuterJoin(transform(stream2)).\
        leftOuterJoin(transform(stream3))
    # clean joined stream
    return joined_stream.map(clean)
```

4. Write a function that updates the global state by every stream:

```
def update_global_state(key_value_pairs):
    def update(new_values, accumulator):
        """
        Counts the number of requests by
        key
        """

        if accumulator is None:
            accumulator = 0

        if not new_values:
            # if not values, return 0 + accumulator
            _ = tuple([0])
```

```python
        elif type(new_values) in (list, tuple,):
            # Assumes a list of lists or similar
            # counts the number of items in every list
            _ = tuple(
                len(r)
                for r in new_values
                if type(r) in (list, tuple,)
            )
        else:
            _ = tuple(0)

        return sum(_, accumulator)

    return key_value_pairs.updateStateByKey(update)
```

5. Next, perform aggregations. Write some code that calls the functions for streams via joining and aggregation. This function also writes the result of every computation in the filesystem:

```python
def join_aggregation(stream1, stream2, stream3):
    """
    Step 1: Joins all streams and return a (key, record)
        dataset
    Step 2: counts all values by column_name
        dataset based on the path
    Step 3: Write updates in the file system.
    """
    path_aggregation = aggregate_by_column(
        stream1, stream2, stream3, column_name='path')
    global_counts = update_global_state(path_aggregation)
    data_dir = os.path.join(
        os.environ['SPARK_DATA'],'streams', 'count_by_request')
    global_counts.saveAsTextFiles(data_dir)
```

6. Initialize the streams and computations:

```python
def consume_records(
        interval=1, host='localhost', port1=9876, port2=12345,
        port3=8765):
    """
```

```
    Create a local StreamingContext with two working
    thread and batch interval
    """
    sc, stream_context = initialize_context(interval=interval)
    stream1 = stream_context.socketTextStream(host, port1)
    stream2 = stream_context.socketTextStream(host, port2)
    stream3 = stream_context.socketTextStream(host, port3)
    join_aggregation(stream1, stream2, stream3)
    stream_context.start()
    stream_context.awaitTermination()


def initialize_context(interval=1, checkpointDirectory='/tmp'):
    """

    Creates a SparkContext, and a StreamingContext object.
    Initialize checkpointing
    """

    spark_context = SparkContext(appName='LogSocketConsumer')
    stream_context = StreamingContext(spark_context, interval)
    stream_context.checkpoint(checkpointDirectory)
    return spark_context, stream_context
```

7. The main function should look like this:

```
def main():
    if 'SPARK_DATA' not in os.environ:
        print('Error. Please define SPARK_DATA variable')
        exit(1)


    parser = argparse.ArgumentParser()
    parser.add_argument(
        '--interval', required=False, default=1.0,
        help='Interval in seconds', type=float)

    parser.add_argument(
        '--port1', required=False, default=9876, help='Port 1', type=int)
```

```
parser.add_argument(
    '--port2', required=False, default=12345, help='Port 2', type=int)

parser.add_argument(
    '--port3', required=False, default=8765, help='Port 3', type=int)


parser.add_argument(
    '--host', required=False, default='localhost', help='Host')

args, extra_params = parser.parse_known_args()

consume_records(
    interval=args.interval, port1=args.port1, port2=args.port2,
    port3=args.port3,  host=args.host)


if __name__ == '__main__':
    main()
```

8. Execute the following command:

```
$YOUR_SPARK_HOME/bin/spark-submit --master local[4] log_socket_consumer.py
--interval 3
```

Introduction to Structured Streaming

Structured Streaming is built on top of the Spark SQL engine. It provides a mechanism to consume live streams in real time and store this data by using the DataFrame and Dataset APIs.

Structured streaming implements checkpointing and write-ahead logs for fault tolerance.

The following diagram shows how structured streaming appends every incoming stream of data to an unbounded (input) table:

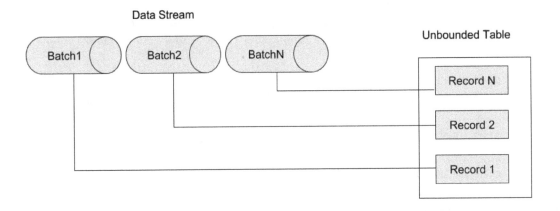

Figure 2.9: Data stream and unbounded table

Result Table and Output Modes in Structured Streaming

A result table is generated by querying the input table. The input table is updated at every interval and will update the result table whenever a query to the table happens.

The most common scenario for structured streaming is to write changed result rows to an external sink.

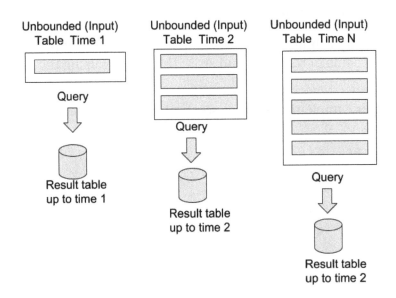

Figure 2.10: Result Table and Output Modes in Structured Streaming

Structured streaming provides the following three output modes:

- **Complete Mode**: The whole updated result table is written to an external storage. The storage connection manager handles the writing process.

- **Append Mode**: New rows appended to the result table are persisted to an external storage. This strategy only works if the existing rows do not change.

- **Update Mode**: Rows that were updated since the last inverval are written to the external storage.

Structured Streaming reads the latest data from the source and updates the result as quickly as possible. Once the result table is updated, the original data is discarded. This model differs from DStreams because it aggregates the data, whereas DStreams expects the user to implement the aggregations.

Exercise 9: Writing Random Ratings

In this exercise, you will create a Python program that writes random ratings to the filesystem. The aim here is to generate data for consumption using structured streaming.

Here are the steps to perform this exercise:

1. Create a Python file named **rating_writer** for the writer, and import the required libraries:

```
from datetime import datetime

import argparse
import random
import time
import os
import csv
import uuid
```

2. Write a function that loads the ratings dataset in memory:

```
users = []
movies = []


def load_data():
    global users
    global movies
    fname = os.path.join(
```

```
            os.environ['SPARK_DATA'], 'ratings.csv'
    )
    with open(fname) as csvfile:
        reader = csv.reader(csvfile, delimiter=',')
        next(reader, None)
        for row in reader:
            users.append(row[0])
            movies.append(row[1])
```

3. Write a function that generates a random rating:

```
def get_rating():
    """
    Returns a user:movie:rating pair
    """
    global users
    global movies
    random.seed(datetime.utcnow().microsecond)
    user = random.choice(users)
    movie = random.choice(movies)
    rating = random.choice([1, 2, 3, 4, 5])
    return [user, movie, rating]
```

4. Write a function that writes random ratings to the filesystem within regular intervals of time:

```
def initialize(interval=0.5):
    """
    Initialize a TCP server that returns a non deterministic
    flow of simulated events to its clients
    """
    load_data()
    export_dir = os.path.join(os.environ['SPARK_DATA'], 'structured')

    if not os.path.exists(export_dir):
        os.makedirs(export_dir)
```

```
print("Writing data in {}".format(export_dir))
while True:
    rt = get_rating()
    fn = '{}.csv'.format(uuid.uuid4())
    fname = os.path.join(export_dir, fn)
    with open(fname, 'w') as f:
        writer = csv.writer(f)
        writer.writerow(rt)
    time.sleep(interval)
```

5. Write a main function that initializes the rating generation:

```
def main():
    if 'SPARK_DATA' not in os.environ:
        print('SPARK_DATA directory or variable not set')
        exit(1)

    parser = argparse.ArgumentParser()

    parser.add_argument(
        '--interval', required=False, default=0.5,
        help='Interval in seconds', type=float)

    args, extra_params = parser.parse_known_args()
    initialize(interval=args.interval)


if __name__ == '__main__':
    main()
```

6. Use the following command that generates random ratings in the local filesystem:

```
python3 rating_writer.py --interval 0.5
```

Exercise 10: Structured Streaming

In this exercise, you will write Python code to use the Structured Streaming API for data consumption in the file system. We'll use the concepts about structured streaming and data consumption from the local file system.

1. Create a Python file named **structured_rating_file_consumer.py** and copy the following code:

```python
from pyspark import SparkContext
from pyspark.sql import SQLContext
from pyspark.sql.types import (
    StructType, StructField, FloatType, StringType, IntegerType
)
from pyspark.sql.streaming import DataStreamReader

import argparse
import os
```

2. Write a function that uses the structured streaming API for consuming ratings from the file system:

```python
def consume_records():
    spark_context = SparkContext(appName='RatingConsumer')
    spark_context.setLogLevel("DEBUG")
    sql_context = SQLContext(spark_context)
    stream_reader = DataStreamReader(sql_context)
    fpath = os.path.join(os.environ['SPARK_DATA'], 'structured')

    fields = [
        StructField('userId', IntegerType(), True),
        StructField('movieId', IntegerType(), True),
        StructField('rating', FloatType(), True),
        StructField('timestamp', StringType(), True),
    ]
    schema = StructType(fields)
    ratings = stream_reader.load(fpath, schema=schema, format='csv')
```

```
user_counts = ratings.groupBy('userId').count()
query = user_counts \
    .writeStream\
    .outputMode('complete')\
    .format('console')\
    .start()
query.awaitTermination()
```

3. Write a main function to parse the streams:

```
def main():
    if 'SPARK_DATA' not in os.environ:
        print('SPARK_DATA directory or variable not set')
        exit(1)

    parser = argparse.ArgumentParser()

    args, extra_params = parser.parse_known_args()
    consume_records()



if __name__ == '__main__':
    main()
```

4. Use the following command that consumes data from the local file system:

```
$YOUR_SPARK_HOME/bin/spark-submit --master local[4] structured_rating_file_
consumer.py
```

Summary

DStreams is a mechanism that allows for streams of live data consumption in real time. It also provides distributed recovery of state and stragglers mitigation. In this lesson, we have learned how to implement a basic workflow for stream consumption of data in real time from a TCP Socket and how to use the most relevant concepts of the Spark Streaming API. We implemented an end-to-end pipeline solution with the concepts that we learned in lessons 1 and 2.

We will explore external data sources and stream integration with other Spark modules in the following lessons.

3

Spark Streaming Integration with AWS

Lesson Objectives

By the end of this lesson, you will be able to:

- Send data to AWS Kinesis and S3 using Python

- Use Python and Spark to consume streams of data from AWS Kinesis

- Use Python and Spark to persist aggregated data in AWS S3

- Implement a cloud-based, end-to-end pipeline

In this lesson, we'll input data from other AWS services. We will integrate Spark with AWS.

Introduction

In *Lesson 1, Introduction to Spark Distributed Processing,* we learned about the basic concepts of Apache Spark and distributed computing. We built standalone Python programs to interact with the Spark cluster by using the RDD API. In *Lesson 2, Introduction to Spark Streaming,* we learned about the Spark Streaming API and how to consume streams of data in real time from a TCP server. In this lesson, we'll learn how to consume live streams of data from AWS Kinesis and store aggregated data in AWS S3.

Spark Integration with AWS Services

Spark Streaming supports integration with external data sources such as AWS Kinesis, Apache Kafka, and Flume. It is also possible to write custom consumers to connect to any other source. Nevertheless, the functionality to consume custom data sources has not been ported to Python yet. Therefore, it will not be covered in this course. In the following sections, we will focus on the consumption of live data from Kinesis and store it after aggregation in AWS S3.

Amazon Kinesis Data Streams is a service in the cloud that provides functionality to capture continuous streams of data in real time. Kinesis can capture terabytes of data per hour, which makes this technology ideal for big data applications such as web analytics, log management, financial transactions, and so on.

Amazon S3 is a cloud-based, key-value storage system. Its API allows writing and reading from any application. It also provides access control and compliance. It is known for its durability. It eases the task of managing data, and is quite secure. S3 is the storage platform of choice for big data analytics.

Previous Requirements

In this section, we'll look at the requirements to get us started with the tasks in this lesson.

AWS Account

To interact with AWS Kinesis and S3, you will need an AWS account and a valid set of access keys. The user associated with your AWS credentials should have access to Kinesis and S3 resources.

> **Note**
>
> For more information about AWS IAM policies, you can visit https://docs.aws.amazon.com/streams/latest/dev/learning-kinesis-module-one-iam.html and https://docs.aws.amazon.com/AmazonS3/latest/dev/s3-access-control.html.

Boto3 Python Library

Boto3 is the AWS SDK for Python. You can use this library to interact with most of the services provided by Amazon, including Kinesis and S3. Boto3 supports Python 2.6.5+, 2.7, and 3.3+.

> **Note**
>
> You can find the project documentation for Boto3 at https://boto3.readthedocs.io/.

You can use the **pip3** command to install boto3:

```
pip3 install boto3
```

AWS Kinesis Data Streams Basic Functionality

A Kinesis data stream is a collection of shards. Each one of these shards represents a unique sequence of records in the stream. Shards have a fixed amount of capacity and they can support up to 2 MB per second for reads and 1 M for writes. The total capacity of a stream is defined by the sum of the capacity of its shards, and it may be modified by increasing or decreasing the number of shards.

Kinesis distributes data across shards. Partition keys are unique strings that are used to allocate data in a given shard. A partition key determines what shard is associated with a given record of data.

The following diagram describes how several applications can send data to Kinesis, and from there, data can be moved to any application, even outside AWS:

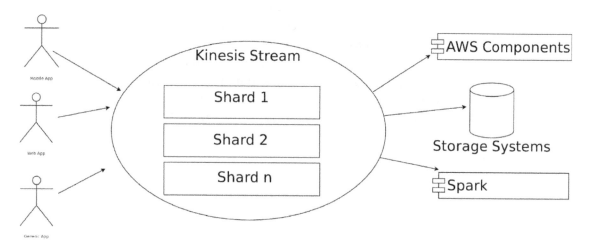

Figure 3.1: Kinesis stream

Integrating AWS Kinesis and Python

In this section, we'll see how to integrate AWS Kinesis and Python. You will write Python code to create, list, and delete Kinesis streams. You'll set up a Kinesis stream for further analysis with Spark Streaming.

Exercise 11: Listing Existing Streams

In this exercise, you'll write Python code to create Kinesis streams.

Here are the steps to perform this exercise:

1. Create a Python file named **list_streams.py** and import the required packages:

```
import argparse
import os
import boto3
import json
```

2. Call the **list_streams** function in the boto library to get a list of streams. Execute the **Kinesis.Client.describe_stream_summary** function:

```
def list_streams(region_name='us-west-2', Limit=10):
    client = boto3.client('kinesis', region_name=region_name)
    result = client.list_streams(Limit=Limit)
    streams = []

    if 'StreamNames' in result:
        for st in result['StreamNames']:
            record = {}
            details = client.describe_stream_summary(
                StreamName=st)['StreamDescriptionSummary']
            record['StreamName'] = st
            record['StreamARN'] = details['StreamARN']
            record['OpenShardCount'] = details['OpenShardCount']
            shards_info = client.list_shards(StreamName=st)
            record['shards'] = shards_info['Shards']
            streams.append(record)
    return streams
```

3. Use the following function to parse the configuration parameters. AWS credentials should be provided as environ variables:

```python
def parse_known_args():

    if 'AWS_ACCESS_KEY_ID' not in os.environ:
        print('Error. Please setup AWS_ACCESS_KEY_ID')
        exit(1)

    elif 'AWS_SECRET_ACCESS_KEY' not in os.environ:
        print('Error. Please setup AWS_SECRET_ACCESS_KEY')
        exit(1)

    parser = argparse.ArgumentParser()
    parser.add_argument('--region_name', required=False,
        help='AWS Region', default='us-west-2')
    parser.add_argument(
        '--Limit', required=False, default=100,
        help='Limit of records returned', type=int)
    args, extra_params = parser.parse_known_args()
    return args, extra_params
```

4. Write a main function that lists all of the streams. List all AWS Kinesis streams associated to a given AWS account using **boto3** library:

```python
def main():
    args, _ = parse_known_args()
    result = list_streams(
        region_name=args.region_name, Limit=args.Limit)
    print(json.dumps(result, indent=2))



if __name__ == '__main__':
    main()
```

5. Set up AWS access keys as environment variables to list the streams:

```
export AWS_ACCESS_KEY_ID=access_key
export AWS_SECRET_ACCESS_KEY=secret_access_key
```

6. This code may be executed with the following command:

```
python3 list_streams.py
```

Exercise 12: Creating a New Stream

In this exercise, you'll write code to create a new Kinesis stream.

Here are the steps to perform this exercise:

1. Create a Python file named **create_stream.py** and copy the following imports:

```
import argparse
import os
import boto3
```

2. Write the **def create_stream()** function that uses the **Kinesis.Client.create_stream** function of **boto3** to create new streams:

```
def create_stream(StreamName=None, ShardCount=1, region_name='us-west-2'):
    assert StreamName is not None

    client = boto3.client('kinesis', region_name=region_name)
    stream = client.create_stream(
        StreamName=StreamName, ShardCount=ShardCount
    )
    return stream
```

Each shard can support reads of up to five transactions per second, up to a maximum data read total of 2 MB per second. A shard can support writes up to 1,000 records per second, up to a maximum data write total of 1 MB per second.

3. Create a stream operation that requires the stream's name and the number of shards. AWS credentials should be provided as environ variable:

```
def parse_known_args():
    if 'AWS_ACCESS_KEY_ID' not in os.environ:
        print('Error. Please setup AWS_ACCESS_KEY_ID')
        exit(1)

    elif 'AWS_SECRET_ACCESS_KEY' not in os.environ:
        print('Error. Please setup AWS_SECRET_ACCESS_KEY')
        exit(1)

    parser = argparse.ArgumentParser()

    parser.add_argument(
            '--region_name', required=False,
            help='AWS Region', default='us-west-2')
    parser.add_argument('--StreamName', required=True, help='Stream name')
```

```
    parser.add_argument(
        '--ShardCount', required=True, help='Number of Shards', type=int)
    args, extra_params = parser.parse_known_args()

    return args, extra_params
```

4. Write a main function to create a new stream using the **boto3** library:

```
def main():
    args, _ = parse_known_args()
    print(
        create_stream(
            StreamName=args.StreamName,
            ShardCount=args.ShardCount, region_name=args.region_name))


if __name__ == '__main__':
    main()
```

5. Use the following command to create a new Kinesis stream:

```
python3 create_stream.py --StreamName test_shards_3 \
    --ShardCount=3 \
    --region_name us-west-2
```

Exercise 13: Deleting an Existing Stream

In this exercise, we'll write Python code to delete an existing stream.

Here are the steps to perform this exercise:

1. Create a Python file named **delete_stream.py** and copy the following imports:

```
import argparse
import os
import boto3
```

2. Use the following boto3 function to delete a Kinesis stream:

```
def delete_stream(StreamName=None, region_name='us-west-2'):
    """
    Executes Kinesis.Client.delete_stream function
    """

    assert StreamName is not None

    client = boto3.client('kinesis', region_name=region_name)
    return client.delete_stream(
```

```
            StreamName=StreamName
    )
```

3. Parse the console arguments. The stream name is required as a console argument. AWS credentials should be provided as environ variables:

```
def parse_known_args():
    if 'AWS_ACCESS_KEY_ID' not in os.environ:
        print('Error. Please setup AWS_ACCESS_KEY_ID')
        exit(1)

    elif 'AWS_SECRET_ACCESS_KEY' not in os.environ:
        print('Error. Please setup AWS_SECRET_ACCESS_KEY')
        exit(1)

    parser = argparse.ArgumentParser()
    parser.add_argument(
        '--region_name', required=False,
        help='AWS Region', default='us-west-2')
    parser.add_argument('--StreamName', required=True, help='Stream name')
    args, extra_params = parser.parse_known_args()
    return args, extra_params
```

4. Write a main function to execute the **boto3** code. It deletes an Amazon Kinesis stream using the **boto3** library:

```
def main():

    args, _ = parse_known_args()
    print(
        delete_stream(
        StreamName=args.StreamName, region_name=args.region_name))


if __name__ == '__main__':
    main()
```

5. Use the following command to remove a Kinesis stream:

```
python3 delete_stream.py --StreamName test_shards_3
```

Exercise 14: Pushing Data to a Stream

In this exercise, we will send events data to Kinesis using Python and the **boto3** library.

Here are the steps to perform this exercise:

1. Create a file named **event_producer_kinesis.py** and copy the following imports:

   ```
   from datetime import datetime

   import argparse
   import boto3
   import json
   import os
   import random
   import time
   import uuid
   ```

2. Use the following code, which chooses between three events at random and appends the current timestamp:

   ```
   def get_line():
       random.seed(datetime.utcnow().microsecond)
       dt = datetime.utcnow()\
       .strftime('%Y-%m-%d %H:%M:%S.%f')

       event = random.choice(['event1', 'event2', 'event3'])    return
   '{};{}'.format(dt, event)
   ```

3. Write the following function, which simulates a non-deterministic value. It returns a random value slightly different than the original interval parameter:

   ```
   def randomize_interval(interval):
       random.seed(datetime.utcnow().microsecond)
       delta = interval + random.uniform(-0.1, 0.9)
       # delay can not be 0 or negative
       if delta <= 0:
           delta = interval
       return delta
   ```

4. Write the following function, which sends data to a Kinesis stream to simulate random delays:

```python
def initialize(StreamName=None, interval=1, region_name='us-west-2'):
    """
    Use Kinesis.Client.put_record function to send data to a kinesis
    stream
    """
    client = boto3.client('kinesis', region_name=region_name)
    while True:
    line = get_line()
        payload = {
            'value': line,
            'timestamp': str(datetime.utcnow()),
            'id': str(uuid.uuid4())
        }

        r = client.put_record(
            StreamName=StreamName,
            Data=json.dumps(payload),
            PartitionKey=str(uuid.uuid4())
        )
        print('Record stored in shard {}'.format(r['ShardId']))
        # Simulates a non deterministic delay
        time.sleep(randomize_interval(interval))
```

5. Parse the console arguments. The stream name should be provided. AWS credentials should be provided as environ variables:

```python
def parse_known_args():
    if 'AWS_ACCESS_KEY_ID' not in os.environ:
        print('Error. Please setup AWS_ACCESS_KEY_ID')
        exit(1)

    elif 'AWS_SECRET_ACCESS_KEY' not in os.environ:
        print('Error. Please setup AWS_SECRET_ACCESS_KEY')
        exit(1)

    parser = argparse.ArgumentParser()
```

```
parser.add_argument(
    '--interval', required=False, default=0.5,
    help='Interval in seconds', type=float)

parser.add_argument(
    '--region_name', required=False,
    help='AWS Region', default='us-west-2')

parser.add_argument('--StreamName', required=True, help='Stream name')


args, extra_params = parser.parse_known_args()

return args, extra_params
```

6. Write a Python main function that initializes the program. List Amazon Kinesis streams associated to a particular AWS account using boto3 library:

```
def main():
    args, extra_params = parse_known_args()
    initialize(
        StreamName=args.StreamName,
        interval=args.interval, region_name=args.region_name)


if __name__ == '__main__':
    main()
```

7. Write a function that sends a stream of simulated events to an AWS Kinesis stream:

```
python3 event_producer_kinesis.py --StreamName event_data --region
us-west-2 --interval 0.2
```

AWS S3 Basic Functionality

Amazon S3 is a storage system where you can store data within resources called **buckets**. You can place any object you want in a bucket and perform operations such as write, read, and delete. The maximum size allowed for every object in a bucket is up to 5 TB.

The following diagram describes how multiple applications write files to a key-value filesystem in the cloud:

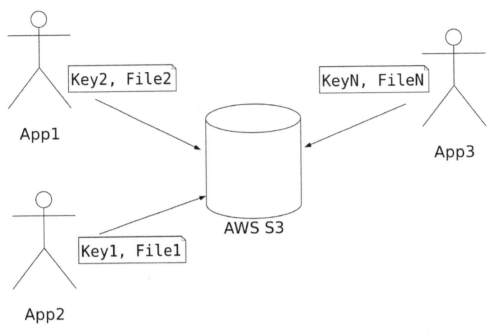

Figure 3.2: Applications and the key-value filesystem in the cloud

Creating, Listing, and Deleting AWS S3 Buckets

In this section, you will write Python code to create, list, and delete AWS S3 buckets. The aim is to create an AWS S3 bucket that you will use to store aggregated data after being processed by Spark streams.

Exercise 15: Listing Existing Buckets

In this exercise, you'll write Python code to list existing buckets.

Here are the steps to perform this exercise:

1. Create a Python file named list_s3_buckets.py and copy the following code:

```
import os
import boto3
```

2. Write a boto3 function to get a list of the available buckets:

```python
def list_buckets():
    """
    Executes the function S3.Client.list_buckets to get a list
    a of buckets by account
    """
    result = []
    client = boto3.client('s3')
    bucket_list = client.list_buckets()
    if 'Buckets' in bucket_list:
        result = [
        b['Name'] for b in bucket_list['Buckets']
        ]

    return result
```

3. Write a simple main function, as no console parameters are required:

```python
def main():
    """
    List AWS S3 buckets using boto3 library
    """
    # AWS credentials should be provided as environ variables
    if 'AWS_ACCESS_KEY_ID' not in os.environ:
        print('Error. Please setup AWS_ACCESS_KEY_ID')
        exit(1)

    elif 'AWS_SECRET_ACCESS_KEY' not in os.environ:
        print('Error. Please setup AWS_SECRET_ACCESS_KEY')
        exit(1)
    for b in list_buckets():
        print(b)


if __name__ == '__main__':
    main()
```

4. Use the following command to execute the code:

```
python3 list_s3_buckets.py
```

Exercise 16: Creating a Bucket

In this exercise, we'll write code to create a bucket.

Here are the steps to perform this exercise:

1. Create a Python file named create_s3_bucket.py and copy the following code:

```python
import argparse
import os
import boto3
```

2. Write a boto3 function to create a new S3 bucket:

```python
def create_bucket(Bucket):
    """
    Executes the function S3.ServiceResource.create_bucket to create
    a new S3 bucket
    """
    client = boto3.client('s3')
    return client.create_bucket(Bucket=Bucket)
```

3. Parse the console commands. The bucket name should be provided by the user:

```python
def parse_known_args():
    # AWS credentials should be provided as environ variables
    if 'AWS_ACCESS_KEY_ID' not in os.environ:
        print('Error. Please setup AWS_ACCESS_KEY_ID')
        exit(1)

    elif 'AWS_SECRET_ACCESS_KEY' not in os.environ:
        print('Error. Please setup AWS_SECRET_ACCESS_KEY')
        exit(1)

    parser = argparse.ArgumentParser()

    parser.add_argument(
        '--region_name', required=False,
        help='AWS Region', default='us-west-2')

    parser.add_argument(
        '--Bucket', required=True, help='S3 Bucket Name'
    )
```

```
args, extra_params = parser.parse_known_args()

return args, extra_params
```

4. Write a main function to create an Amazon S3 bucket:

```
def main():
    """
    Creates an Amazon S3 Bucket using boto3 library
    """
    args, _ = parse_known_args()
    print(
        create_bucket(args.Bucket))


if __name__ == '__main__':
    main()
```

5. Use the following command to execute the code:

```
python3 create_s3_bucket.py --Bucket testuniquebucket
```

> **Note**
>
> Keep in mind that the name you choose for the bucket should be unique. It has to be unique to all accounts because the S3 naming space is shared across all AWS users.

Exercise 17: Deleting a Bucket

In this exercise, we'll write Python code to delete a bucket.

Here are the steps to perform this exercise:

1. Create a Python file named **delete_s3_bucket.py** and import the required packages:

```
import argparse
import os
import boto3
```

2. Write a boto3 function to delete a given bucket:

```python
def delete_bucket(bucket=None):
    """
    Executes S3.Client.delete_bucket to delete a given bucket
    """
    client = boto3.client('s3')
    return client.delete_bucket(Bucket=bucket)
```

3. Parse the console arguments. Bucket is a required field. AWS credentials should be provided as environ variables:

```python
def parse_known_args():
    if 'AWS_ACCESS_KEY_ID' not in os.environ:
        print('Error. Please setup AWS_ACCESS_KEY_ID')
        exit(1)

    elif 'AWS_SECRET_ACCESS_KEY' not in os.environ:
        print('Error. Please setup AWS_SECRET_ACCESS_KEY')
            exit(1)

    parser = argparse.ArgumentParser()

    parser.add_argument(
        '--region_name', required=False,
        help='AWS Region', default='us-west-2')

    parser.add_argument(
        '--Bucket', required=True, help='S3 Bucket Name'
    )

    args, extra_params = parser.parse_known_args()

    return args, extra_params
```

4. Write a main function that creates an Amazon Kinesis stream using the **boto3** library:

```python
def main():
    args, _ = parse_known_args()
    print(
        delete_bucket(args.Bucket))
```

```
if __name__ == '__main__':
    main()
```

5. Use the following command to execute the code:

```
python delete_s3_bucket.py --Bucket testuniquebucket
```

Kinesis Streams and Spark Streams

Spark provides functionality to consume data from Kinesis streams. A Kinesis stream shard is processed by one input DStream at a time. Spark uses multiple threads to read from multiple shards using only one DStream.

The current position of the stream is stored in DynamoDB, along with checkpointing information. This data is used as a mechanism for failure recovery. If Spark can not find any information about the last processed record, it will attempt to consume data from the latest record available (**InitialPositionInStream.LATEST**) or from the first record in the stream (**InitialPositionInStream.TRIM_HORIZON**).

The following diagram shows how Spark consumes live streams of data from AWS Kinesis and checkpoints information about computational state in DynamoDB:

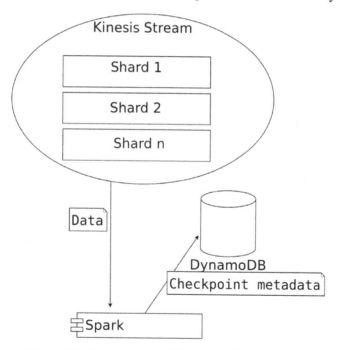

Figure 3.3 Live streams of data and checkpointing

The following code uses the **pyspark.streaming.kinesis** library to create a DStream from a Kinesis stream:

```
from pyspark.streaming.kinesis import KinesisUtils, InitialPositionInStream


stream = KinesisUtils.createStream(
    stream_context, 'EventLKinesisConsumer', StreamName, endpoint,
    region_name, InitialPositionInStream.LATEST, interval)
```

You should include the Kinesis dependency explicitly when running **spark-submit**:

```
$YOUR_SPARK_HOME/bin/spark-submit --packages org.apache.spark:spark-
streaming-kinesis-asl_2.11:2.3.1
```

Activity 4: AWS and Spark Pipeline

In this activity, you will write Python code to consume and aggregate data from a Kinesis stream. The aggregated data will be stored in AWS S3.

The aim of this activity is to use AWS components to consume and store aggregated data using Spark streaming.

The following diagram describes the workflow you are going to implement:

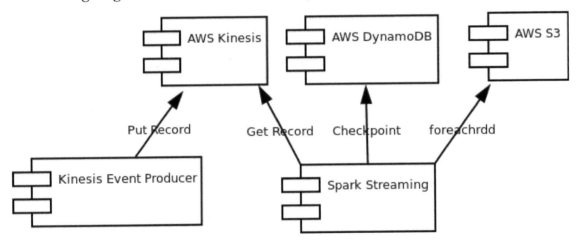

Figure 3.4: AWS and Spark workflow of this activity

In the first part of this activity, you will use the Python program you built in the previous exercise under *Exercise 11, Pushing Data to a Stream*, to send event data to AWS Kinesis.

In the second part of this activity, you will write a Python program that uses Spark Streaming to consume data in real time from AWS Kinesis. You will apply transformations and aggregations to the incoming data and finally store the aggregated data in AWS S3.

Here are the steps to perform this activity:

1. Create a new Kinesis stream.

2. Verify whether the stream was successfully created.

3. Push event data to the stream.

4. Create an S3 bucket. Remember that you need to provide a unique name because the S3 namespace is shared across all accounts.

5. Verify whether the bucket was created.

6. Create a Python file named `kinesis_event_consumer.py` and import the required libraries.

7. Write a function that parses a Kinesis message and returns a Python dictionary.

8. Write a function to update the global state of the stream.

9. Perform data aggregation. Write code to perform a series of transformations to finally apply a reduction by key in order to count the number of events by event type.

10. Write data to AWS S3. Every RDD can be stored as text in an S3 bucket by using the boto3 library.

11. Next, look at consuming records. Write a function that creates a Spark stream from Kinesis, which processes the incoming records and performs some aggregations and transformation. This function also calls foreachRDD to persist aggregated information in AWS S3.

12. Write a function to initialize the Spark and Streaming context objects.

13. Parse the console arguments. Users should provide the bucket and Kinesis stream names. Additional parameters are optional.

14. Write a main function that will start the Kinesis stream consumption.

15. Use a command to initialize the process.

> **Note**
>
> The solution for this activity can be found at Page No. 113.

You can now modify the Kinesis consumer application to consume another stream from a TCP socket, join both streams, and perform basic aggregations.

Summary

In this lesson, we have learned how to integrate Spark with AWS services such as Kinesis and S3. We also learned how to use Spark Streaming functionalities such as foreachRDD to store aggregated data in AWS S3. In the following lesson, we will learn how to integrate Spark Streaming with the machine learning extension.

Spark Streaming, ML, and Windowing Operations

Lesson Objectives

By the end of this lesson, you will be able to:

- Use the Spark machine learning library

- Build a collaborative filtering model for movie recommendations

- Build a system that suggest movies in real time by using Spark streams and machine learning

- Apply windowing operations to live streams of data

This chapter concludes this book by describing how we can use the streaming feature in collaboration with the machine learning functionality using MLib library.

Introduction

In the last three lessons, we learned about the most relevant concepts regarding Spark and Spark Streaming. We performed practical exercises to learn how to use RDD and the SQL APIs, and we also learned how to consume live streams of data from TCP servers and from AWS Kinesis.

In this lesson, we will learn how to integrate Spark Streaming with the machine learning functionality by implementing a system to recommend movies in real time.

Spark Integration with Machine Learning

MLlib is Spark's machine learning library, and it provides functionality that allows for the usage of common algorithms and data processing mechanisms at scale in an easy way. The following table describes the most relevant features of this library:

Algorithms	Featurization	Pipelines	Persistence	Utilities
Classification Regression Clustering Collaborative filtering	Feature extraction Transformation Dimensionality reduction Selection	Construction Evaluation Tuning ML Pipelines	Import and export of algorithms, models and Pipelines	Linear algebra Statistics Data manipulation.

Figure 4.1: Features of MLlib

The MovieLens Dataset

We will use the reduced version of the MovieLens dataset in this lesson. It contains about 100,000 ratings and 1,300 tag applications that have been applied to 9,000 movies by 700 users.

> **Note**
>
> Further information about this dataset can be found at https://grouplens.org/datasets/movielens/.

We built a Python program in *Exercise 4, Downloading the Reduced Version of the MovieLens Dataset*, which downloads this dataset. The following command will execute that program and will download the MovieLens dataset in the location specified by the **SPARK_DATA** environment variable:

```
python3 dowload_movielens.py
```

Introduction to Recommendation Systems and Collaborative Filtering

Recommendation systems provide the ability to identify and recommend similar items. This ability is very important because it may influence purchase habits and generate an increase or decrease in revenue. The complexity of performing recommendation operations in big datasets prevents the implementation of very good solutions in production due to their high computational requirements.

There are multiple types of recommendation systems. Their performance and complexity vary from one type to another; nevertheless, all of these systems have similar behaviors: they produce a list of similar items that can help a customer make a decision. We will focus the remainder of this lesson on a particular type of recommendation known as collaborative filtering.

An introduction to recommendation systems and collaborative filtering can be found in a white paper that has been released under the creative commons license and can be downloaded from https://github.com/maigfrga/nt-recommend/blob/master/documentation/recsys_intro.pdf.

Collaborative filtering is a technique used in recommendation systems for two purposes:

- Generating a list of similar items

- Generating predictions for specific items

There are several approaches for collaborative filtering. The most common are as follows:

- User-based

- Item-based

- Matrix factorization

- Alternating least squares (Spark approach)

Collaborative filtering combines preferences of similar users to generate predictions and recommendations. The following steps describe the algorithm's behavior:

1. Build a user-item matrix.

2. Compute similarity among users by using statistical correlations.

3. Build a subset of similar users.

4. Generate a prediction or a list of items.

A data structure known as the user-item matrix is used to store all ratings for all users. The following table shows an example of this matrix:

	Item 1	Item 2	Item 3	Item 4	..:.	Item n
User 1	3	2			...	3
User 2	1		4	2	...	3
...	...	...	...	...	...	...
User N	5	3		1	...	4

Figure 4.2: User-item matrix

Exercise 18: Collaborative Filtering and Spark

In this exercise, you'll create a Python-based recommendation system in Spark for the MovieLens dataset. You'll make use of the basic concepts of Spark's machine learning functionality.

Here are the steps to perform this exercise:

1. Create a Python file named **spark_recommender.py** and copy the following imports:

```
from pyspark import SparkContext
from pyspark.sql import DataFrameReader, SQLContext
from pyspark.sql.types import (
    StructType, StructField, FloatType, StringType, IntegerType
)
from pyspark.ml.evaluation import RegressionEvaluator
from pyspark.ml.recommendation import ALS

import os
```

2. Create a Python class and define functions that expect the **SparkContext** and **SQLContext** objects:

```
class MovieRecommender(object):
    def __init__(self, sc, sqlctx, data_dir=None):
        # spark context
        self.sc = sc

        # sql context
        self.sqlctx = sqlctx
```

```
    if data_dir is not None:
        self.data_dir = data_dir
    elif 'SPARK_DATA' in os.environ:
        self.data_dir = os.environ['SPARK_DATA']
    else:
        print('SPARK_DATA directory or variable not set')
        exit(1)
    self.initialize()


def initialize(self):
    self.load_datasets()
    self.build_model()
```

3. Write a function that uses the Spark DataFrame and SQL functionality to load the ratings dataset in memory:

```
def load_datasets(self):
    """
    Loads movielens dataset from a given location
    """
    reader = DataFrameReader(self.sqlctx)

    fields = [
        StructField('userId', IntegerType(), True),
        StructField('movieId', IntegerType(), True),
        StructField('rating', FloatType(), True),
        StructField('timestamp', StringType(), True),
    ]
    schema = StructType(fields)
    self.ratings = reader.csv(
        os.path.join(self.data_dir, 'ratings.csv'),
        schema=schema,
        header=True, mode="DROPMALFORMED"
    )
```

4. Now, build a machine learning model. Write a function that creates a collaborative filtering model by splitting the MovieLens dataset into two datasets: one for predictions and the other for testing:

```
def build_model(self):
    (self.training, self.test) = self.ratings.randomSplit([0.8, 0.2])

    self.als = ALS(
        maxIter=5, regParam=0.01,
        userCol="userId", itemCol="movieId", ratingCol="rating",
        coldStartStrategy="drop")
    self.model = self.als.fit(self.training)
```

5. Write a function that evaluates the performance of the model by using the Root Mean Square error over the test set:

```
def test_model(self):
    # Evaluate the model by computing the RMSE on the test data
    predictions = self.model.transform(self.test)
    evaluator = RegressionEvaluator(
        metricName="rmse", labelCol="rating",
    predictionCol="prediction")
    rmse = evaluator.evaluate(predictions)
    print("Root-mean-square error = " + str(rmse))
```

6. Write a function that updates the ratings dataset with additional ratings:

```
def update_model(self, data):
    fields = [
        StructField('userId', IntegerType(), True),
        StructField('movieId', IntegerType(), True),
        StructField('rating', FloatType(), True),
        StructField('timestamp', StringType(), True),
    ]
    schema = StructType(fields)
    df = self.sqlctx.createDataFrame(data, schema=schema)
    self.ratings = self.ratings.union(df)
    self.build_model()
```

7. Write a function that returns a list of recommendations for all the users, passed as parameters:

```
def get_recommendations(self, users, n_items=10):
    return self.model.recommendForUserSubset(users, n_items)
```

8. Use the **run_model** function, which will initialize the SparkContext and SQLContext objects and create a recommender object for the MovieLens dataset:

```python
def run_model():
    sc = SparkContext(appName='MovieLens Recommender')
    sc.setLogLevel("DEBUG")
    sql_context = SQLContext(sc)
    recommender = MovieRecommender(sc, sql_context)
    recommender.test_model()
    # get a list of top 3 users
    user_list = [
        (r['userId'],) for r in
        recommender.ratings.select('userId').distinct().limit(3).collect()
    ]

    fields = [
        StructField('userId', IntegerType(), True),
    ]
    schema = StructType(fields)

    users = sql_context.createDataFrame(user_list, schema)
    print(users)

    recommendations = recommender.get_recommendations(users)
    print(recommendations)

if __name__ == '__main__':
    run_model()
```

9. Execute the program by typing the following command into your console:

```
$YOUR_SPARK_HOME/bin/spark-submit  --master local[4]  spark_recommender.py
```

Troubleshooting

You may get an error if you don't have NumPy on your system:

```
ImportError: No module named numpy
```

The following command may be used to install the required library:

```
sudo pip3 install numpy
```

Exercise 19: Creating a TCP Server that Publishes User Ratings

In this exercise, you will create a Python TCP server that generates user ratings. The aim here is to build a mechanism to send ratings to Spark Streaming for the real-time recommendation of movies.

Here are the steps to perform this exercise:

1. Create a Python file named **user_producer.py** with the libraries required to build a TCP server:

   ```
   from datetime import datetime

   import argparse
   import random
   import time
   import socket
   import os
   import csv
   ```

2. Write a function that will load the ratings from the MovieLens dataset in memory:

   ```
   users = []
   movies = []

   def load_data():
       global users
       global movies
       fname = os.path.join(
           os.environ['SPARK_DATA'], 'ratings.csv'
       )
       with open(fname) as csvfile:
           reader = csv.reader(csvfile, delimiter=',')
           next(reader, None)
           for row in reader:
               users.append(row[0])
               movies.append(row[1])
   ```

3. Write a function that returns a random **user:movie:rating** pair:

```python
def get_line():
    global users
    global movies
    random.seed(datetime.utcnow().microsecond)
    user = random.choice(users)
    movie = random.choice(movies)
    rating = random.choice([1, 2 , 3, 4, 5 ])
    return '{}:{}:{}\n'.format(user, movie, rating).encode('utf-8')
```

4. Write a function that simulates a random delay. The function must return a random value slightly different than the original interval parameter:

```python
def randomize_interval(interval):
    random.seed(datetime.utcnow().microsecond)
    delta = interval + random.uniform(-0.1, 0.9)
    # delay can not be 0 or negative
    if delta <= 0:
        delta = interval
    return delta
```

5. Write a function that creates a TCP server. The TCP server must return a non-deterministic flow of simulated events to its clients:

```python
def initialize(port=9876, interval=0.5):
    load_data()
    sock = socket.socket(socket.AF_INET, socket.SOCK_STREAM)
    server_address = ('localhost', port)
    sock.bind(server_address)
    sock.listen(5)
    print("Listening at {}".format(server_address))
    try:
        connection, client_address = sock.accept()
        print('connection from', client_address)
        while True:
```

```
            line = get_line()
            connection.sendall(line)
            time.sleep(randomize_interval(interval))
        except Exception as e:
            print(e)

        finally:
            sock.close()
```

6. Write a main function that initializes the program:

```
def main():
    if 'SPARK_DATA' not in os.environ:
        print('SPARK_DATA directory or variable not set')
        exit(1)

    parser = argparse.ArgumentParser()
    parser.add_argument(
            '--port', required=False, default=9876,
            help='Port', type=int)

    parser.add_argument(
            '--interval', required=False, default=0.5,
            help='Interval in seconds', type=float)
    args, extra_params = parser.parse_known_args()
    initialize(port=args.port, interval=args.interval)


if __name__ == '__main__':
    main()
```

7. Use the following command to execute the Python program:

```
python3 user_producer.py --interval 0.5 --port 9876
```

Exercise 20: Spark Streams Integration with Machine Learning

In this exercise, you will create a Spark stream consumer that will read live ratings from a TCP server and update a machine learning model in real time. The aim here is to integrate Spark streams with machine learning.

Here are the steps to perform this exercise:

1. Create a Python file named **stream_recommender.py** and import the required libraries:

```python
from pyspark import SparkContext
from pyspark.sql import SQLContext
from pyspark.streaming import StreamingContext
from spark_recommender import MovieRecommender
from datetime import datetime
import argparse
```

2. Write a function that transforms every incoming rating and returns a dictionary. Here, it'll parse every movie rating:

```python
def parse_rating(msg):

    values = msg.split(':')

    return {
        'userId': int(values[0]),
        'movieId': int(values[1]),
        'rating': float(values[2]),
        'timestamp':  datetime.utcnow().strftime('%Y-%m-%d %H:%M:%S.%f')
    }
```

3. Write a function that updates the collaborative filtering model with upcoming ratings:

```python
def update_model(rdd, recommender):
    print('updating recommender model')
    recommender.update_model(rdd.collect())
    print('total ratings: {}'.format(recommender.ratings.count()))
```

4. Write a function that consumes live ratings by using windowing operations. This updates the collaborative filtering model with the data collected in every window. It must collect movie ratings from users and updates a machine learning model for movies recommendations. This Stream uses windowing operations to send batches of data for the model update instead of recomputing the model every time that a new RDD arrives:

```
def consume_records(
        interval=1, windowLength=4, slideInterval=2,
        port=9876, host='localhost'):
    spark_context = SparkContext(appName='RatingConsumer')
    spark_context.setLogLevel("DEBUG")
    sql_context = SQLContext(spark_context)
    recommender = MovieRecommender(spark_context, sql_context)
    stream_context = StreamingContext(spark_context, interval)
    stream = stream_context.socketTextStream(host, port)

    ratings = stream.window(windowLength, slideInterval).map(parse_rating)
    ratings.foreachRDD(lambda rdd: update_model(rdd, recommender))

    stream_context.start()
    stream_context.awaitTermination()
```

5. Write a main function that parses the console arguments and initializes the stream's consumption:

```
def main():
    parser = argparse.ArgumentParser()
    parser.add_argument(
        '--interval', required=False, default=2.0,
        help='Interval in seconds', type=float)

    parser.add_argument(
        '--windowLength', required=False, default=4,
        help='Window Length', type=float)

    parser.add_argument(
        '--slideInterval', required=False, default=2,
        help='slideInterval', type=float)
```

```
parser.add_argument(
    '--port', required=False, default=9876,
    help='Port', type=int)

parser.add_argument(
    '--host', required=False, default='localhost', help='Host')

args, extra_params = parser.parse_known_args()
consume_records(
    interval=args.interval, windowLength=args.windowLength,
    slideInterval=args.slideInterval, port=args.port, host=args.host)


if __name__ == '__main__':
    main()
```

6. Use the following command to start a stream for listening user ratings in real time:

```
$YOUR_SPARK_HOME/bin/spark-submit --master local[4]  stream_recommender.py
\
--interval 2 --windowLength 4 --slideInterval 2 --port 9876
```

Activity 5: Experimenting with Windowing Operations

In this activity, we'll build on the preceding exercise. We'll experiment with different windowLength and slideInterval values for windowing operations. We'll read live ratings from a TCP Server and update a machine learning model in real time.

Here are the steps to perform this exercise:

1. Create a Python file named **spark_recommender.py** and import the required libraries, namely **SparkContext**, **SQLContext**, **StreamingContext**, **MovieRecommender**, **datetime**, and **argparse**.

2. Write a function that parses every movie ratings, and returns user ID, movie ID, ratings, and timestamp.

3. Write a function that updates recommender model with ratings collected from live stream. Print the total ratings.

4. Write a function that collects movie ratings from users and updates a machine learning model for movies recommendations. We'll have **windowlLengt=5** and **slideInterval=2**.

5. Write a main function that parses the arguments consisting of interval in seconds, window length, slide interval, host and port.

6. Execute the program by using your console.

> **Note**
>
> The solution for this activity can be found at Page No. 117.

Summary

In this lesson, we have learned about the basics of the Spark machine learning library. We developed a collaborative filtering model for movie recommendations and we integrated this model with Spark streaming. We concluded this course with a brief introduction to Structured Streaming.

So, in a nutshell, you've written your own Python programs that can interact with Spark. You've implemented data stream consumption using Apache Spark. You've recognized common operations in Spark to process known data streams. You've written code to push and consume information. And, finally, you've integrated streams with the machine learning API.

Appendix A

About

This section is included to assist the students to perform the activities present in the course. It includes detailed steps that are to be performed by the students to complete and achieve the objectives of the course.

Lesson 1: Introduction to Spark Distributed Processing

Activity 1: Statistical Operations on Books

Solution:

1. Open the file you've used for the exercise (**book_analysis_act_b1.py** in this case).

2. Define a function by the name statistics, and import operator and statistics:

```
def statistics(book):
    import operator
    import statistics
```

3. Next, get the average word length. Use the function mentioned in the *Prerequisites* section of this activity. Print the word length.

```
# average
print(book.take(2))
avg =  book.map(lambda x: len(x[0]) ).reduce(operator.add) / book.
count()
print("Stats for book {}".format(book.name()))
print('Average word length: {}'.format(avg))
```

4. Next, get the standard deviation of average word length. Use the function mentioned in the *Prerequisites* section of this activity. Print it.

```
dev = statistics.stdev(
        book.map(
            lambda x: len(x[0])).collect()
    )
print('Standard Deviation: {}'.format(dev))
```

5. Print the most five frequent words in each book by using **book.takeOrdered(5, key=lambda k: -k[1])**.

```
print('Top 5 most frequent words:')
print(book.takeOrdered(5, key=lambda k: -k[1]))
```

Lesson 2: Introduction to Spark Streaming

Activity 2: Building a Simple TCP Spark Stream Consumer

Solution:

1. Create a Python file named **event_stream_consumer.py** and import the required libraries:

```
from pyspark import SparkContext
from pyspark.streaming import StreamingContext
from datetime import datetime
import argparse
```

2. Next, we'll write a function to parse a string event. The TCP server pushes stream messages in the format **"timestamp;event\n"**. The following code parse strings in this format and returns a dictionary:

```
def parse_entry(msg):
    """

    Event TCP sends sends data in the format
    timestamp:event\n
    """

    values = msg.split(';')
    return {
        'dt': datetime.strptime(
            values[0], '%Y-%m-%d %H:%M:%S.%f'),
        'event': values[1]
    }
```

3. Write a function that applies a series of transformations and actions to aggregate streams of data by event type:

```
def aggregate_by_event_type(record):
    """

    Step 1. Maps every entry to a dictionary.
    Step 2. Transform the dataset in a set of
        tuples (event, 1)
    Step 3: Applies a reduction by event type
        to count the number of events by type
        in a given interval of time.
    """

    return record.map(parse_entry)\
        .map(lambda record: (record['event'], 1))\
        .reduceByKey(lambda a, b: a+b)
```

4. Write a function that uses the Spark streams API to pull data from a socket in a given interval of time:

```python
def consume_records(
        interval=1, host='localhost', port=9876):
    # Create a local StreamingContext with two working
    #    thread and batch interval of 1 second
    spark_context = SparkContext(appName='LogSocketConsumer')
    stream_context = StreamingContext(spark_context, interval)
    stream = stream_context.socketTextStream(host, port)

    # counts number of events
    event_counts = stream.map(parse_entry)\
        .map(lambda record: (record['event'], 1))\
        .reduceByKey(lambda a, b: a+b)
    event_counts.pprint()
    stream_context.start()
    stream_context.awaitTermination()
```

5. Write a simple Python 3 function that parses console arguments to provide an interface to users:

```python
def main():
    parser = argparse.ArgumentParser()
    parser.add_argument(
        '--interval', required=False, default=1.0,
        help='Interval in seconds', type=float)

    parser.add_argument(
        '--port', required=False, default=9876,
        help='Port', type=int)

    parser.add_argument(
        '--host', required=False, default='localhost', help='Host')

    args, extra_params = parser.parse_known_args()
    consume_records(
        interval=args.interval, port=args.port, host=args.host)


if __name__ == '__main__':
    main()
```

6. Use the following command that connects to the TCP socket, pulling a live stream of data from port 9875, and building chunks of data that arrive in an interval within 3 seconds:

```
$YOUR_SPARK_HOME/bin/spark-submit --master local[2] event_stream_consumer.
py --interval 3 --port 9875
```

The following screenshot shows how Spark Streaming aggregates events every 3 seconds:

```
- - - - - - - - - - - - - - - - - - - - - - - - - - - - - - - -
Time: 2018-07-07 22:01:15
- - - - - - - - - - - - - - - - - - - - - - - - - - - - - - - -
(u'event2', 3)
(u'event3', 1)
(u'event1', 3)


- - - - - - - - - - - - - - - - - - - - - - - - - - - - - - - -
Time: 2018-07-07 22:01:18
- - - - - - - - - - - - - - - - - - - - - - - - - - - - - - - -
(u'event2', 4)
(u'event3', 2)
(u'event1', 2)


- - - - - - - - - - - - - - - - - - - - - - - - - - - - - - - -
Time: 2018-07-07 22:01:21
- - - - - - - - - - - - - - - - - - - - - - - - - - - - - - - -
(u'event2', 1)
(u'event3', 2)
(u'event1', 4)
```

Activity 3: Consuming Event Data from Three TCP Servers

Solution:

1. Create a Python file and import the required libraries, namely **datetime**, **SparkContext**, **StreamingContext**, and **argparse**:

```
from datetime import datetime

from pyspark import SparkContext
from pyspark.streaming import StreamingContext


import argparse
```

2. Write a function by which Event TCP sends data in the format `timestamp:event\n`:

```python
def parse_entry(msg):
    """
    Event TCP sends sends data in the format
    timestamp:event\n
    """
    values = msg.split(';')
    return {
        'dt': datetime.strptime(
            values[0], '%Y-%m-%d %H:%M:%S.%f'),
        'event': values[1]
    }
```

3. Write a function that maps every entry to a dictionary, transforms the dataset in a set of tuples (event, 1), and applies a reduction by event type to count the number of events by type in a given interval of time:

```python
def aggregate_by_event_type(record):
    """
    Step 1. Maps every entry to a dictionary.
    Step 2. Transform the dataset in a set of
        tuples (event, 1)
    Step 3: Applies a reduction by event type
        to count the number of events by type
        in a given interval of time.
    """
    return record.map(parse_entry)\
        .map(lambda record: (record['event'], 1))\
        .reduceByKey(lambda a, b: a+b)
```

4. Write a function that receives as parameter a DStream and applies an update function in order to keep aggregated information about event types counts:

```python
def update_global_event_counts(key_value_pairs):
    """
    Function that receives as parameter a DStream
    and applies an update function in order to keep
    aggregated information about event types counts.
    """
    def update(new_values, accumulator):
        if accumulator is None:
```

```
            accumulator = 0
        return sum(new_values, accumulator)

    return key_value_pairs.updateStateByKey(update)
```

5. Write a function that parses, joins, and aggregates three streams:

```
def aggregate_joined_stream(pair):
    key = pair[0]
    values = [val for val in pair[1][0] if val is not None]
    if pair[1][1] is not None:
        values.append(pair[1][1])
    key = 'global_count_{}'.format(key)
    return(key, sum(values))


def join_aggregation(stream1, stream2, stream3):
    key_value_pairs = stream1.map(parse_entry)\
        .map(lambda record: (record['event'], 1))
    running_event_counts = update_global_event_counts(key_value_pairs)
    running_event_counts.pprint()

    key_value_pairs2 = stream2.map(parse_entry)\
        .map(lambda record: (record['event'], 1))
    running_event_counts2 = update_global_event_counts(key_value_pairs2)
    running_event_counts2.pprint()

    key_value_pairs3 = stream3.map(parse_entry)\
        .map(lambda record: (record['event'], 1))
    running_event_counts3= update_global_event_counts(key_value_pairs3)
    running_event_counts3.pprint()

    n_counts_joined = running_event_counts.leftOuterJoin(running_event_
counts2)\
        .leftOuterJoin(running_event_counts3)
    n_counts_joined.pprint()
    n_counts_joined.map(aggregate_joined_stream).pprint()
```

6. Write a function that creates a local StreamingContext with two working thread and batch interval:

```python
def consume_records(
        interval=1, host='localhost', port1=9876, port2=12345,
port3=23456):
    """
    Create a local StreamingContext with two working
    thread and batch interval
    """
    sc, stream_context = initialize_context(interval=interval)
    stream1 = stream_context.socketTextStream(host, port1)
    stream2 = stream_context.socketTextStream(host, port2)
    stream3 = stream_context.socketTextStream(host, port3)
    join_aggregation(stream1, stream2, stream3)
    stream_context.start()
    stream_context.awaitTermination()
```

7. Write a function that creates a SparkContext, and a StreamingContext object. Initialize checkpointing as well:

```python
def initialize_context(interval=1, checkpointDirectory='/tmp'):
    """
    Creates a SparkContext, and a StreamingContext object.
    Initialize checkpointing
    """
    spark_context = SparkContext(appName='LogSocketConsumer')
    stream_context = StreamingContext(spark_context, interval)
    stream_context.checkpoint(checkpointDirectory)
    return spark_context, stream_context
```

8. Write a main function to parse console parameters and initialize streams:

```python
def main():
    parser = argparse.ArgumentParser()
    parser.add_argument(
        '--interval', required=False, default=2.0,
        help='Interval in seconds', type=float)

    parser.add_argument(
        '--windowLength', required=False, default=4,
        help='Window Length', type=float)
    parser.add_argument(
```

```
        '--slideInterval', required=False, default=2,
        help='slideInterval', type=float)

    parser.add_argument(
        '--port', required=False, default=9876,
        help='Port', type=int)

    parser.add_argument(
        '--host', required=False, default='localhost', help='Host')

    args, extra_params = parser.parse_known_args()
    consume_records(
        interval=args.interval, windowLength=args.windowLength,
        slideInterval=args.slideInterval, port=args.port, host=args.host)


if __name__ == '__main__':
    main()
```

Lesson 3: Spark Streaming Integration with AWS

Activity 4: AWS and Spark Pipeline

Solution:

1. Create a new Kinesis stream.

    ```
    python3 create_stream.py --StreamName event_data \
        --ShardCount=3 \
        --region_name us-west-2
    ```

2. Verify whether the stream was successfully created:

    ```
    python3 list_streams.py
    ```

3. Push event data to the stream:

    ```
    python3 event_producer_kinesis.py --StreamName event_data --region
    us-west-2 --interval 0.2
    ```

4. Create an S3 bucket. Remember that you need to provide a unique name because the S3 namespace is shared across all accounts.

    ```
    python3 create_s3_bucket.py --Bucket testuniquebucket
    ```

5. Verify whether the bucket was created:

```
python3 list_s3_buckets.py
```

6. Create a Python file named **kinesis_event_consumer.py** and import the required libraries:

```python
from datetime import datetime
from glob import glob
from pyspark import SparkContext
from pyspark.streaming import StreamingContext
from pyspark.streaming.kinesis import KinesisUtils,
InitialPositionInStream

import argparse
import boto3
import json
import os
```

7. Write a function that parses a Kinesis message and returns a Python dictionary.

```python
def parse_entry(record):
    """
    Event TCP sends sends data in the format
    timestamp:event\n
    """
    msg = record['value']
    values = msg.split(';')

    # remove \n character if exists

    event = values[1].replace('\n', '')

    return {
        'dt': datetime.strptime(
            values[0], '%Y-%m-%d %H:%M:%S.%f'),
        'event': event,
        'timestamp': datetime.strptime(
            record['timestamp'], '%Y-%m-%d %H:%M:%S.%f')
    }
```

8. Write a function to update the global state of the stream:

```python
def update_global_event_counts(key_value_pairs):
    def update(new_values, accumulator):
        if accumulator is None:
            accumulator = 0
        return sum(new_values, accumulator)

    return key_value_pairs.updateStateByKey(update)
```

9. Perform data aggregation. Write code to perform a series of transformations to finally apply a reduction by key in order to count the number of events by event type:

```python
def aggregate_by_event_type(record):
    """
    Step 1. Maps every entry to a dictionary.
    Step 2. Transform the dataset in a set of
            tuples (event, 1)
    Step 3: Applies a reduction by event type
            to count the number of events by type
            in a given interval of time.
    """

    return record\
        .map(lambda x: json.loads(x))\
        .map(parse_entry)\
        .map(lambda record: (record['event'], 1))\
        .reduceByKey(lambda a, b: a+b)
```

10. Write data to AWS S3. Every RDD can be stored as text in an S3 bucket by using the boto3 library:

```python
def send_record(rdd, Bucket):
    """
    If rdd size is greater than 0, store the
    data as text in S3
    """

    if rdd.count() > 0:
```

```
client = boto3.client('s3')
data_dir = os.path.join(
        os.environ['SPARK_DATA'],
        'streams', 'kinesis_{}'.format(datetime.utcnow().timestamp()))
rdd.saveAsTextFile(data_dir)
for fname in glob('{}/part-0000*'.format(data_dir)):
        client.upload_file(fname, Bucket, fname)
```

11. Next, look at consuming records. Write a function that creates a Spark stream from Kinesis, which processes the incoming records and performs some aggregations and transformation. This function also calls **foreachRDD** to persist aggregated information in AWS S3.

```
def consume_records(
        interval=1, StreamName=None, region_name='us-west-2',
    Bucket=None):
    assert StreamName is not None

    endpoint = 'https://kinesis.{}.amazonaws.com/'.format(region_name)

    sc, stream_context = initialize_context(interval=interval)
    sc.setLogLevel("INFO")
    stream = KinesisUtils.createStream(
        stream_context, 'EventLKinesisConsumer', StreamName, endpoint,
        region_name, InitialPositionInStream.LATEST, interval)

    # counts number of events
    event_counts = aggregate_by_event_type(stream)
    global_counts = update_global_event_counts(event_counts)
    global_counts.pprint()
    # Sends data to S3
    global_counts.foreachRDD(lambda rdd: send_record(rdd, Bucket))
    stream_context.start()
    stream_context.awaitTermination()
```

12. Write a function to initialize the Spark and Streaming context objects:

```
def initialize_context(interval=1, checkpointDirectory='/tmp'):
    """

    Creates a SparkContext, and a StreamingContext object.
    Initialize checkpointing
    """
```

```
spark_context = SparkContext(appName='EventLKinesisConsumer')
stream_context = StreamingContext(spark_context, interval)
stream_context.checkpoint(checkpointDirectory)
return spark_context, stream_context
```

13. Parse the console arguments. Users should provide the bucket and Kinesis stream names. Additional parameters are optional

```
def parse_known_args():
    # AWS credentials should be provided as environ variables
    if 'AWS_ACCESS_KEY_ID' not in os.environ:
        print('Error. Please setup AWS_ACCESS_KEY_ID')
        exit(1)
    elif 'AWS_SECRET_ACCESS_KEY' not in os.environ:
        print('Error. Please setup AWS_SECRET_ACCESS_KEY')
        exit(1)

    if 'SPARK_DATA' not in os.environ:
        print('Error. Please define SPARK_DATA variable')
        exit(1)

    parser = argparse.ArgumentParser()

    parser.add_argument(
        '--interval', required=False, default=1.0,
        help='Interval in seconds', type=float)

    parser.add_argument(
        '--region_name', required=False,
        help='AWS Region', default='us-west-2')

    parser.add_argument('--StreamName', required=True, help='Stream name')

    parser.add_argument(
        '--Bucket', required=True, help='S3 Bucket Name'
    )

    args, extra_params = parser.parse_known_args()

    return args, extra_params
```

14. Write a main function that will start the Kinesis stream consumption:

```
def main():
    args, extra_params = parse_known_args()
    consume_records(
        interval=args.interval, StreamName=args.StreamName,
        Bucket=args.Bucket, region_name=args.region_name)


if __name__ == '__main__':
    main()
```

15. Use a command to initialize the process:

```
$YOUR_SPARK_HOME/bin/spark-submit   --packages org.apache.spark:spark-
streaming-kinesis-asl_2.11:2.3.1 \
  --master local[4] kinesis_event_consumer.py \
  --interval 3 --StreamName event_data \
  --Bucket uniquebucketname
```

Lesson 4: Spark Streaming, ML, and Windowing Operations

Activity 5: Experimenting with Windowing Operations

Solution:

1. Create a Python file, and import the required libraries, namely **SparkContext**, **SQLContext**, **StreamingContext**, **MovieRecommender**, **datetime**, and **argparse**:

```
from pyspark import SparkContext
from pyspark.sql import SQLContext
from pyspark.streaming import StreamingContext
from spark_recommender import MovieRecommender
from datetime import datetime
import argparse
```

2. Write a function that parses every movie ratings, and returns user ID, movie ID, ratings, and timestamp:

```
def parse_rating(msg):
    """

    Parse every movie rating
    """

    values = msg.split(':')
```

```
    return {
        'userId': int(values[0]),
        'movieId': int(values[1]),
        'rating': float(values[2]),
        'timestamp':  datetime.utcnow().strftime('%Y-%m-%d %H:%M:%S.%f')
    }
```

3. Write a function that updates recommender model with ratings collected from live stream. Print the total ratings:

```
def update_model(rdd, recommender):
    """

    Update recommender model with ratings collected from live stream
    """

    print('updating recommender model')
    recommender.update_model(rdd.collect())
    print('total ratings: {}'.format(recommender.ratings.count()))
```

4. Write a function that collects movie ratings from users and updates a machine learning model for movies recommendations. We'll have **windowlLengt=5** and **slideInterval=2**:

```
def consume_records(
        interval=1, windowLength=5, slideInterval=3,
        port=9876, host='localhost'):
    spark_context = SparkContext(appName='LogSocketConsumer')
    spark_context.setLogLevel("DEBUG")
    sql_context = SQLContext(spark_context)
    recommender = MovieRecommender(spark_context, sql_context)
    stream_context = StreamingContext(spark_context, interval)
    stream = stream_context.socketTextStream(host, port)

    ratings = stream.window(windowLength, slideInterval).map(parse_rating)
    ratings.foreachRDD(lambda rdd: update_model(rdd, recommender))

    stream_context.start()
    stream_context.awaitTermination()
```

5. Write a main function:

```python
def main():
    parser = argparse.ArgumentParser()
    parser.add_argument(
        '--interval', required=False, default=2.0,
        help='Interval in seconds', type=float)

    parser.add_argument(
        '--windowLength', required=False, default=4,
        help='Window Length', type=float)

    parser.add_argument(
        '--slideInterval', required=False, default=2,
        help='slideInterval', type=float)

    parser.add_argument(
        '--port', required=False, default=9876,
        help='Port', type=int)

    parser.add_argument(
        '--host', required=False, default='localhost', help='Host')

    args, extra_params = parser.parse_known_args()
    consume_records(
        interval=args.interval, windowLength=args.windowLength,
        slideInterval=args.slideInterval, port=args.port, host=args.host)


if __name__ == '__main__':
    main()
```

6. Execute the program via your console:

```
$YOUR_SPARK_HOME/bin/spark-submit --master local[4]  stream_recommender.py \
--interval 2 --windowLength 4 --slideInterval 2 --port 9876
```

Index

About

All major keywords used in this book are captured alphabetically in this section. Each one is accompanied by the page number of where they appear.

A

agents, 52-53
aggreation, 48
aggregate, 4, 35, 40, 43,
    46, 49-50, 56-57, 84
aggregated, 4, 45, 50,
    52, 67-68, 78, 84-86
aggregates, 49-50, 61
algorithm, 91
algorithms, 5, 90
amazon, 9, 68-69,
    74, 77, 81-82
amazons, 68
analyses, 23, 27
analysis, 10, 14, 17,
    19, 23, 27, 70
analytics, 68
analyzers, 4
apache, 2, 4-8, 12,
    21, 68, 84, 102
appname, 20, 24, 26, 39,
    44, 48, 58, 64, 95, 100
arbritrary, 21
argparse, 41-42, 47,
    50, 52, 54-55, 58,
    61, 63-65, 70-76,
    80-82, 96, 98-101
average, 19

B

batches, 39, 100
benchmark, 23
berkeley, 39
bingbot, 52
boolean, 22
broadcast, 8
bucket, 77-83, 85
--bucket, 80-83
buckets, 77-79

C

center, 3
centers, 2
charles, 14
checkpoint, 44, 48, 58
chrome, 52
clients, 42-43, 62, 97
cluster, 1-2, 5-8, 20,
    32, 36, 44, 68
clustered, 2
cogroup, 44
collection, 2, 5, 8-9,
    12, 27, 30, 69
command, 8, 21, 43, 49,
    54, 59, 63, 65, 69,
    71, 73-74, 79, 81, 83,
    86, 90, 95, 98, 101
commands, 80
comparison, 39
compatible, 52
components, 4-5, 84
compute, 50, 91
computes, 22
computing, 2-3, 20, 68, 94
concept, 7
concepts, 4, 10, 20,
    27, 32, 35-36, 51,
    64-65, 68, 90, 92
connect, 39, 68
connecting, 35-36
connection, 5-6, 8, 42,
    53-54, 61, 97-98

D

dataframe, 27,
    30-31, 59, 93
dataframes, 1, 4-5,
    27, 30, 32
dataset, 7-13, 15-16, 18,
    27-31, 40, 45-46, 50,
    56-57, 59, 61, 90, 92-96
datasets, 1, 4-5, 7, 9,
    12-14, 20, 27-28, 32,
    39, 90-91, 93-94
decode, 14, 17, 24, 29
definitive, 44
delays, 41, 43, 76
delimiter, 62, 96
delivers, 2
delivery, 2
dependency, 84
depicts, 7
deploy, 6
deployed, 2
deployment, 5, 7
developed, 102
deviation, 19
devices, 3
diagram, 4, 7, 39, 47,
    60, 69, 78, 83-84
dickens, 14
dstream, 39-40, 45,
    49-50, 83-84
dstreams, 5, 38-40,
    46, 61, 65
dynamodb, 83

E

encode, 41, 54, 97
endeavor, 36
endpoint, 84
engine, 39, 59
environ, 28-30, 57-58,
    62-65, 71-72, 74, 76,
    79-80, 82, 93, 96, 98
esperanza, 52

F

fibonacci, 22-23
filter, 9, 11-12, 15-18,

22, 25, 30, 44, 56
findall, 55
firefox, 52
flatmap, 12, 15, 17, 25, 44
floattype, 64, 92-94
foreachrdd, 85-86, 100
frequency, 16-17, 25

G

generator, 25
generic, 16
genres, 30-31
github, 91
global, 45-46, 49-50, 52,
    55-57, 61-62, 85, 96-97
graphx, 5
groupby, 65
groupbykey, 12
grouped, 51
grouplens, 28, 90
groups, 39

H

hadoop, 7
hamlet, 17-18, 26
--host, 48, 59, 101

I

innovation, 39
instances, 6, 51, 54
integers, 10
integrate, 5, 67, 70,
    86, 90, 99
interact, 1, 4, 9, 20,
    32, 68-69, 102
interface, 20, 43, 51
interfaces, 5
item-based, 91
itemcol, 94

J

joined, 46, 49, 56
joining, 13, 57

K

keeping, 45
key-value, 13, 45-46,
    56, 68, 78
keyword, 21
kinesis, 67-77, 82-86, 90
kubernetes, 7

L

labelcol, 94
lambda, 9, 11-13, 15-22,
    25, 31, 40, 45-46,
    49, 56, 100
libraries, 43, 50, 61,
    85, 96, 99, 101
library, 5, 69-71, 73-75,
    77, 79, 81-82, 84-85,
    89-90, 95, 102
license, 91
localhost, 42, 46, 48, 53,
    57, 59, 97, 100-101

M

machine, 4-6, 86, 89-90,
    92, 94, 99-102
maigfrga, 14, 17, 26, 28, 91
makedirs, 62
manager, 6, 61
managing, 68
mapped, 12
mapping, 20
map-reduce, 40
mathworld, 22
matrix, 91-92

maxiter, 94
metadata, 27, 44
metricname, 94
migrate, 5
mitigation, 39, 65
movieid, 30-31, 64,
    93-94, 99
movielens, 28-29,
    90, 92-96
movilens, 28
mozilla, 52
mycontent, 2-3

N

namespace, 85
nested, 22, 24
normalize, 15, 17, 24-25
numeric, 20
nutshell, 102

O

outputmode, 65

P

packages, 47, 55, 70, 81
paradigm, 22
params, 42, 48, 54, 59,
    63, 65, 71, 73-74,
    77, 81-82, 98, 101
parser, 42, 47-48,
    54, 58-59, 63, 65,
    71-74, 76-77, 80-82,
    98, 100-101
parses, 43, 49-50,
    55, 85, 100-102
payload, 76
pipeline, 3, 35-36,
    51, 65, 67, 84
platform, 68

policies, 68
--port, 42-43, 47-49,
    54, 58-59, 98, 101
pprint, 40, 45-46, 49
pyspark, 8, 20, 23,
    29-31, 39, 41, 44, 47,
    55, 64, 84, 92, 99
python, 1, 4-5, 8, 10-12,
    20-21, 23-24, 27-29, 32,
    35-36, 41, 43, 47, 49-50,
    54-55, 61, 63-64, 67-75,
    77-81, 83-85, 90, 92,
    96, 98-99, 101-102

Q

queries, 1, 30-32
querying, 60

R

randint, 53
random, 21, 41, 43, 52-53,
    61-63, 75-76, 96-97
ratingcol, 94
recovery, 7, 38-39,
    44, 65, 83
recsys, 91
recursion, 22
refactor, 23
regparam, 94
resilience, 44
resilient, 1, 4-5, 7,
    12, 14, 32, 39
resources, 6, 68, 77

S

safari, 52
scientists, 3
script, 24, 29
search, 55
sendall, 42, 54, 98
shardcount, 72-73
shardid, 76
shards, 69-70, 72-74, 83
socket, 39, 41-43, 52-55,
    59, 65, 86, 96-97
sockets, 35
spliting, 94
sqlcontext, 64, 92,
    95, 99-101
sqlctx, 92-94
stateful, 44, 47, 50
stragglers, 39, 65
stream, 35, 39-40,
    42-50, 53, 55-58, 60,
    64-65, 69-70, 72-77,
    82-86, 97, 99-102
streamarn, 70
streaming, 4-5, 32,
    35-36, 39, 41, 44-47,
    52, 55, 59-61, 64-65,
    67-68, 70, 84-86,
    89-90, 96, 99, 102
streamname, 70,
    72-74, 76-77, 84
streams, 5, 35-36, 38-39,
    43, 46-52, 56-57, 59,
    65, 67-72, 77-78, 83,
    86, 89-90, 99, 102
strftime, 41, 75, 99
string, 13-14, 21-22,
    31, 41, 43
strings, 21, 43, 69
stringtype, 64, 92-94
strptime, 40

structtype, 64, 92-95
structure, 27, 92
structured, 5, 27,
    59-62, 64-65, 102

T

takesample, 12
technique, 38, 91
techniques, 23
technology, 68
techrpts, 39
temporary, 31, 44
terabytes, 68
terminal, 49-50
testing, 94
text-based, 20
textfile, 9
therefore, 21, 68
thread, 48, 50, 58
threads, 83
timestamp, 40-41, 43, 50,
    64, 75-76, 93-94, 99, 101
tokenize, 15, 17, 24-25
tokenizing, 24
tokens, 15-16, 25
transform, 1, 16, 31-32,
    40, 44, 56, 94
transforms, 46, 50, 99
tuples, 40, 50

U

unbounded, 60
uniform, 41, 75, 97
urllib, 14, 17, 24, 28-29
urlopen, 14, 17, 24, 29
usercol, 94
utcnow, 23, 41, 53,
    62, 75-76, 97, 99

V

variable, 21, 28-29, 58,
    63, 65, 72, 90, 93, 98

W

webserver, 53
wolfram, 22
workflow, 43, 47, 65, 84
writerow, 63

CPSIA information can be obtained
at www.ICGtesting.com
Printed in the USA
BVHW011326181218
535884BV00009B/113/P

9 781789 808810